AF426615

CULTIVATING UNDERSTANDING

Nurturing Diversity, Equity, and Inclusion in Higher Education

Rafael Class II

Copyright © 2023

All rights reserved. No part of this publication may be reproduced, stored, or transmitted in any form or by any means, electronic, mechanical, photocopying, recording, scanning, or otherwise without written permission from Rafael Class II or the publisher. It is illegal to copy this book, post it to a website, or distribute it by any other means without permission.

Purpose

This comprehensive book aims to equip higher education professionals with a deep understanding of diversity, equity, and inclusion and how to cultivate these values within their institutions. It provides practical guidance and insights into creating an environment that respects and values all individuals, while also fostering an inclusive learning and working experience.

By covering key topics such as understanding bias, inclusive teaching and learning, recruiting diverse faculty and staff, and building an inclusive campus climate, this book serves as a roadmap for transforming higher education institutions into inclusive spaces where students, faculty, and staff can thrive.

Through the exploration of strategies, tools, and best practices, readers will gain insights into creating awareness, fostering intercultural competence, and promoting equity and access in higher education. The book also delves into challenges such as navigating dialogues on controversial topics, engaging allies, and assessing progress to ensure sustainability.

With case studies and practical examples, this book enables readers to apply the concepts discussed to real-world situations. Built on research and experiences from diverse institutions, it offers a comprehensive resource for higher education professionals seeking to create lasting change and cultivate a culture of diversity, equity, and inclusion.

Whether you are an administrator, faculty member, staff member, or student, this book provides valuable insights and actionable steps to foster understanding and create an inclusive environment that celebrates diversity in the higher education sector.

Introduction

Regarding higher education, diversity, equity, and inclusion (DEI) are integral components for creating welcoming and supportive learning environments. DEI initiatives help bridge gaps in understanding, empower students, and embrace the unique backgrounds and perspectives that each individual brings. To ensure that DEI efforts are successful, higher education institutions must prioritize creating a culture of understanding and respect.

Creating a culture of understanding and respect is crucial to successful DEI initiatives. Higher education institutions must strive to create an environment of acceptance, not just tolerance. By fostering a sense of different backgrounds and identities, students can better appreciate the perspectives of their peers. This understanding should extend beyond the classroom and into the workplace, the dorms, and the greater college community.

Meaningful DEI initiatives should also focus on empowering students and faculty. This includes providing students and faculty with resources and support to help them succeed. It also means providing opportunities for growth and advancement. Higher education institutions can help create a more equitable and inclusive environment by focusing on empowering students and faculty.

It is important to note that DEI initiatives are not simply a one-time effort but should instead be an ongoing exploration process. Educators should develop practices that foster an environment of dialogue and understanding, such as hosting discussions and debates, creating student-led initiatives, and providing resources and training on DEI topics. It may also be beneficial to allow the students to share their stories and experiences to understand better and support each other. Additionally, institutions should ensure students have equitable access to resources and opportunities, such as support services, scholarships, and internships.

Educators should strive to create an environment of inclusion and understanding. This means providing students and faculty access to resources promoting dialogue and understanding. Educators should also facilitate discussions and debates related to DEI topics and provide resources and training on those topics. Student-led initiatives can also be beneficial in fostering an understanding of DEI.

In addition to dialogue and understanding, ensuring students have equitable access to resources and opportunities is essential. This includes, but is not limited to, support services, internships, and scholarships. Allowing students to share their stories and experiences can help create a more inclusive environment. It is also necessary for institutions to provide faculty with resources and support to ensure their success. Finally, institutions should provide opportunities for both students and faculty to grow and advance.

By nurturing a culture of diversity, equity, and inclusion, higher education institutions can create an environment where individuals feel valued and respected. Through understanding and dialogue, we can create a more equitable and inclusive society that allows all individuals.

Creating an environment of diversity, equity, and inclusion is necessary in higher education institutions to ensure everyone feels welcome and respected. This can be done by providing educational programs and resources to encourage dialogue and understanding. Such resources should be available to faculty and students so they can gain the skills needed to create an equitable and inclusive society.

In addition to resources, institutions should provide faculty with the necessary support to ensure they can succeed. This can include access to mentorship opportunities, professional development programs, and guidance to help them navigate the institution. It is also essential for faculty to have a platform to share their stories and experiences, so they can help create a more inclusive environment.

Finally, for students and faculty to grow, institutions should provide opportunities for advancement. These can range from research fellowships to scholarships, internships, and awards. Additionally, institutions should support faculty to help them navigate the promotion process and receive recognition for their work. This will show support for the faculty and create a more equitable and inclusive environment.

CONTENTS

CHAPTER ONE

1.1 Understanding Diversity, Equity, and Inclusion

Exploring the Impact of Higher Education is the key to unlocking countless opportunities and success for individuals worldwide. By understanding the impact of diversity, equity, and inclusion on higher education, we can create an environment where everyone is afforded the same opportunities.

In higher education, diversity is about creating an environment where all students can learn and grow. This means building a space where students of all backgrounds feel safe and accepted. Equity ensures that everyone has access to the same resources and that no one is disadvantaged. This involves removing barriers that might prevent students from accessing resources and opportunities. Finally, inclusion means creating an environment where everyone feels respected and valued. This includes fostering an environment of understanding and acceptance.

Delving into the impact of diversity, equity, and inclusion on higher education can help create an environment where everyone has the same opportunities to succeed. By recognizing the importance of these concepts in higher education, we can ensure that all students have access to the same resources and opportunities.

Diversity, equity, and inclusion in higher education can help bridge the gap between students from different backgrounds. It emphasizes the importance of inclusivity and provides resources and support to help all students succeed. Removing cultural and social barriers opens the door for all students to reach their full potential.

In addition, diversity, equity, and inclusion in higher education can also benefit faculty and staff. It helps create a more diverse and inclusive workplace, promoting a culture of respect and understanding. This can help foster collaboration, increase productivity, and can help to create a more positive and supportive work environment.

Ultimately, diversity, equity, and inclusion in higher education can help create a more equitable and inclusive environment for all students. By recognizing the importance of these concepts, we can ensure that all students have access to the same resources and opportunities, giving them an equal chance to succeed.

Diversity, equity, and inclusion also help to promote a sense of community and collaboration among students. Creating an environment that supports and celebrates diversity allows students to learn from each other, share ideas, and develop relationships that foster meaningful dialogue and mutual understanding. This shared experience leads to greater respect for one another and greater academic success.

Creating a diverse and equitable environment encourages students to share their unique perspectives and engage in meaningful dialogue. This dialogue can help to build a sense of community and collaboration among students. As students learn from each other, they can become more aware of the needs and perspectives of their peers, leading to more tremendous respect for one another. A sense of belonging and trust can be fostered by including all.

In turn, this improved learning environment can lead to increased academic success. By creating a culturally competent space responsive to the unique needs and perspectives of all members of the academic community, students can feel more comfortable in their learning environment. This will help ensure that everyone is allowed to reach their full academic potential.

1.2 The Significance of Diversity, Equity, and Inclusion in Higher Education

Over the past decade, diversity, equity, and inclusion (DEI) have become increasingly important in higher education. DEI is based on the idea that everyone should be valued and respected, regardless of their background, abilities, or beliefs. This concept is fundamental in higher education, ensuring all students access the same resources, opportunities, and respect. Additionally, DEI helps create a safe environment for all students, essential for learning and growth.

DEI is based on the idea that everyone should be treated with respect and given equal opportunities regardless of race, gender, religious beliefs, age, or other factors. Higher education is a key area where this concept should be applied, as students come from various backgrounds and should have access to the same resources. This is especially important for minority students, who might have less access to resources and opportunities than other students.

DEI also promotes a safe and welcoming environment for all students, essential for a successful learning experience. It encourages a sense of belonging in the school community and can help reduce the feeling of isolation or alienation that some students may experience. This helps create an environment conducive to learning where all students feel comfortable and respected. Additionally, DEI helps foster a sense of community and encourages collaboration and communication among all students, which can improve academic performance.

By implementing DEI policies in higher education, institutions can provide a more diverse and equitable environment for all students. Such policies include increasing access to education for minority and underrepresented students, creating more inclusive curricula, and providing resources and support for students from all backgrounds. Through these policies, institutions can promote a more inclusive and equitable learning environment, which is essential for the success of all students.

Diversity, Equity, and Inclusion (DEI) policies in higher education aim to create an equitable and inclusive learning environment for all students. These policies are designed to provide a more diverse and equitable education experience for students from underrepresented and minority backgrounds and all other students. This includes better access to education, more inclusive curriculums, and the necessary resources and support for all students.

DEI policies attempt to create an environment where all students feel comfortable, respected, and included. This helps reduce instances of isolation or alienation that some students may feel, creating an environment conducive to learning. Additionally, DEI policies can foster a sense of community and collaboration among all students, which can help to improve academic performance. By implementing DEI policies, higher education institutions can promote an equitable and inclusive learning environment, which is essential for the success of all students.

Diversity, Equity, and Inclusion (DEI) policies are crucial for higher education institutions to create a safe, welcoming, and affirming learning environment. These policies help ensure that all students are given the same opportunities to succeed, regardless of their background, race, ethnicity, religion, gender, and more. In addition to providing equitable access to resources, DEI also helps create an environment where students from different backgrounds can learn from each other and understand each other's perspectives. This can lead to a deeper understanding of the material and greater empathy and respect for one another.

Finally, DEI is essential for higher education because it helps create a more equitable and just society in the long run. By providing access to education and resources for all students, higher education institutions can foster an understanding of different cultures and backgrounds, leading to more tolerance and acceptance. This is especially important for underprivileged students, as it gives them the tools and resources they need to achieve their goals and succeed. This can ultimately lead to a more just and equitable society.

Part I: Building Blocks of a Diverse and Inclusive Environment

CHAPTER TWO

2.0 Creating Awareness and Disrupting Bias

When it comes to creating awareness and disrupting bias, it is essential to understand the underlying concepts. A preference is an inclination or prejudice toward one group over another. This can favor one gender, race, religion, ethnic group, or another group. It is essential to identify such biases to understand how they impact our decision-making and relationships.

To recognize and address bias, it is essential first to understand the different types of bias. Implicit biases are unconscious attitudes and stereotypes that we have developed over time. Explicit biases, on the other hand, are conscious beliefs and attitudes that we are aware of. It is essential to recognize both types of bias to address them effectively.

Once we have identified any existing biases, we can then begin to work on disrupting them. This involves challenging our preferences as well as those of others. We can do this by engaging in meaningful conversations and examining the root causes of discrimination. We can also look for opportunities to celebrate diversity and foster inclusion. Doing so can create a more equitable and inclusive environment for everyone.

The way to start disrupting biases is to ensure our language is respectful and inclusive. This includes being aware of the impact of our words and how others might interpret them. We should also be conscious of the stereotypes and assumptions associated with certain groups and challenge them whenever possible. Creating a culture of acceptance and inclusion requires engaging in meaningful conversations about diversity and listening to different perspectives. This could involve taking the time to learn about other cultures and the challenges faced by marginalized groups. Creating safe spaces for people to express themselves and be heard is also essential. Doing so can create an environment where everyone feels respected and valued for their unique experiences and perspectives.

Learning about different cultures, religions, and backgrounds can open our eyes to different perspectives and help us build empathy. It can also help us better understand the challenges faced by marginalized groups. For example, by learning about the history of racism and oppression, we can better understand the impact this has had on people of color. Similarly, by learning about the struggles of the LGBTQ+ community, we can better understand their unique experiences and challenges.

Through education and understanding, we can create an environment where everyone is respected and valued for their experiences. We can also create safe spaces for people to express themselves and be heard without fear of judgment or discrimination.

We must listen and understand each other's perspectives and work together to create a world where everyone is accepted and free to be their true selves.

Finally, we can take steps to create greater understanding and empathy by educating ourselves on different cultures, religions, and backgrounds. This can help make greater compassion and respect for each other. By doing this, we can work to create an environment that is free of discrimination and prejudice and where everyone is seen and heard.

2.1 Recognizing Implicit Bias

The concept of implicit bias has existed since the early 20th century, but it has only recently become a significant focus in psychology. Implicit biases are unconscious beliefs, attitudes, and stereotypes that affect our decisions and behavior. They differ from explicit biases, which are conscious beliefs we are aware of and can easily articulate.

Implicit biases are deeply rooted in our culture and often so ingrained that we are unaware of them. In recent years, there has been a growing awareness of people's implicit biases and how they can affect our actions and decisions.

Studies have shown that implicit biases can significantly impact decision-making, especially in hiring practices, education, criminal justice, and healthcare. For example, research has shown that people are more likely to hire someone with a similar background, regardless of qualifications. This type of implicit bias can lead to a lack of diversity and equality in organizations. Similarly, implicit bias can lead to an uneven distribution of school resources and disparities in healthcare and criminal justice.

Recognizing implicit bias has led to an increased focus on understanding the nature of these biases and how to address them. This has included research into how implicit bias affects decision-making and the development of strategies to reduce or eliminate its effects. As more attention is given to this issue, it is hoped that it will lead to more equitable outcomes in all areas of life.

Implicit bias can be found in many areas of our lives, from hiring practices to school funding and criminal justice. It can be challenging to recognize, as it is often unconscious, and many people are unaware of its existence. This has led to research into how implicit bias affects decision-making and what strategies can reduce or eliminate its effects.

Hiring practices are among the most prominent areas in which implicit bias exists. People are more likely to hire someone with a similar background, even if they are not the most qualified candidate. This type of implicit bias can lead to a lack of diversity and equality in organizations and a lack of opportunity for those without the same background.

Implicit bias can also be seen in the workplace. Hiring managers often have implicit biases that impact their decisions. Even if a qualified candidate from an underrepresented group applies for a position, the hiring manager may be more likely to hire someone with a background similar to their own. This type of implicit bias can lead to a lack of diversity and equality in organizations and a lack of opportunity for those without the same background.

The effects of implicit bias can also be seen in other facets of life, such as education and healthcare. Schools in affluent areas may have more resources, leading to disparities in educational opportunities for those in less privileged neighborhoods. In healthcare, implicit bias can lead to unequal treatment, access, and quality of care. In the criminal justice system, people from certain demographics may be more likely to be arrested and convicted, and receive harsher sentences than those from other backgrounds. Therefore, implicit bias can significantly impact our lives and society.

Our upbringing, environment, and culture can form implicit biases. They can also be shaped through our interactions with others, such as coworkers, peers, and family members. It's essential to recognize that we all have implicit biases, which can have a powerful impact on our thoughts and behavior.

We must become aware of our implicit biases and work to reduce their influence on our daily lives. This can be done by examining our behaviors and attitudes, actively engaging in self-reflection, and dialoguing with others. We can also vigorously challenge our implicit biases through education and training. By recognizing and addressing our implicit biases, we can create a more equitable and inclusive society.

2.2 Disrupting Bias in Decision-Making

Decisions are an integral part of life. We make decisions for ourselves, our families, and our communities. But often, decisions are made based on bias. This bias can be conscious or unconscious and can lead to decisions that are unfair and unjust. To combat this, organizations are making a concerted effort to disrupt bias in decision-making.

Organizations are implementing various strategies to reduce bias in decision-making. One of these strategies is to increase the diversity of people involved in the decision-making process. This can be achieved by having a more diverse team of decision-makers, including people from different backgrounds and walks of life.

Another strategy is to promote transparency and accountability. This can be done by setting up processes and procedures to ensure that decisions are made objectively, and everyone involved is held accountable. Additionally, organizations are developing new decision-making tools and technologies, such as artificial intelligence and machine learning, to help reduce bias in decision-making. These tools can be used to analyze data to create more objective and equitable outcomes.

Ultimately, organizations are looking for ways to remove the influence of bias in decision-making. By implementing strategies such as increasing diversity on decision-making teams, promoting transparency and accountability, and utilizing new tools and technologies, organizations can create more equitable and just decisions.

This disruption is achieved through the introduction of data-driven decision-making. By leveraging data, decisions can be made that are evidence-based, objective, and free from bias. This data can be used to gain insights into how decisions are being made and what potential biases may be at play. Organizations can then use this data to inform their decision-making processes and achieve more equitable outcomes.

Organizations are increasingly leveraging data-driven decision-making to drive their operations. This shift is driven by the need to remove potential bias from the decision-making process. Data-driven decisions allow organizations to make decisions that are supported by evidence and are objective. This helps to create more equitable outcomes, as decisions can be made from a neutral perspective.

Data-driven decision-making allows organizations to gain a better understanding of how decisions are being made. This can help identify potential biases and provide insights into how decisions are impacted by individual preferences. This data can then be used to inform decision-making processes and achieve more equitable outcomes. Organizations can implement strategies such as increasing diversity on decision-making teams, promoting transparency and accountability, and utilizing new tools and technologies to facilitate more just and equitable decisions.

Additionally, organizations are promoting diversity and inclusion initiatives. Having a diverse and inclusive workforce can help reduce bias in decision-making. People from different backgrounds can bring varied perspectives and insights that can be valuable in making decisions. It is also important to ensure that everyone has an equal say in the decision-making process. This can help ensure that everyone's opinion is heard and taken into consideration. By fostering a more equitable decision-making environment, organizations can disrupt bias and achieve more equitable outcomes.

Organizations are taking steps to reduce bias in decision-making and create a more equitable environment. This includes promoting diversity and inclusion initiatives. Having a diverse workforce can bring different perspectives and insights to the decision-making process. It is also important to ensure that everyone has an equal say in these processes. This helps ensure that all voices are heard and every opinion is considered.

Furthermore, organizations are implementing strategies to increase transparency and accountability. This can include providing access to data and information so that decisions are based on facts, rather than personal preferences or biases. Technology can also be used to help create more just and equitable decisions. By using tools such as artificial intelligence and machine learning, organizations can analyze data to identify potential biases and ensure that decisions are fair and equitable.

2.3 Strategies for Fostering Awareness and Inclusion

Creating an inclusive workplace is essential for any business. To ensure a safe and welcoming environment, employers can implement various strategies. One of the most important is providing employees with comprehensive training and education. This should include information about the company's values and policies, as well as resources for those who experience discrimination or harassment.

In addition to educating employees, employers can also foster an atmosphere of inclusion by offering support to those who feel threatened or discriminated against. This could include ensuring that there are clear anti-discrimination policies in place, as well as providing counseling services to those in need. With these measures in place, employers can create an environment that is both comfortable and respectful for all employees.

Another strategy to promote awareness and inclusion is to create an inclusive environment. This means setting a tone of respect and understanding and providing equal opportunities for all employees.

Employers should also participate in diverse initiatives, such as offering mentorship programs and hiring from underrepresented communities. Additionally, employers should recognize and celebrate diversity in the workplace, and provide employees with the tools and resources they need to succeed.

Creating an inclusive environment is key to fostering a sense of belonging for all employees. This means implementing workplace policies that ensure everyone feels respected, valued, and heard. Employers should also ensure that all employees have equal access to opportunities, regardless of their race, gender, or any other factor. Additionally, employers should provide employees with the resources they need to succeed, such as training programs, mentorship opportunities, and career development tools.

Furthermore, employers should actively participate in diversity initiatives to create a workplace that celebrates and respects differences. This could include hosting diversity events, providing resources for underrepresented communities, or offering workshops on cultural awareness. By doing so, employers can ensure that all employees feel safe and accepted in the workplace.

Creating a diverse workplace starts with open communication. Employers should ensure that their employees feel comfortable speaking up and sharing their experiences. They should also actively listen to their employees and be open to hearing different points of view. This can help create an atmosphere of mutual respect and understanding.

Employers should also provide resources for underrepresented communities and offer workshops on cultural awareness. This can help create a safe and supportive environment where employees from all backgrounds feel respected and accepted. Additionally, employers can host diverse events to celebrate the unique backgrounds of their employees and promote inclusion in the workplace.

By taking steps to create a workplace that celebrates and respects differences, employers can foster an environment that is more inclusive and supportive. This can help ensure that all employees feel safe and accepted in the workplace.

Finally, employers should work to foster a culture of open communication. This can be achieved by encouraging employees to share their experiences, feedback, and suggestions. Employers should also actively listen to their employees and be open to hearing different perspectives. By fostering an environment of open dialogue and mutual respect, employers can create a more inclusive workplace.

CHAPTER THREE

3.0 Inclusive Teaching and Learning

Inclusive teaching and learning are about creating an atmosphere of acceptance and respect, where each student is treated with dignity. This means all students are given the same learning opportunities, regardless of their backgrounds, beliefs, or abilities. Inclusive teaching and learning also encourage educators to provide differentiated instruction so that all students can access the material in a way that is meaningful to them.

Inclusive teaching and learning also seeks to eliminate barriers preventing students from learning. This can include things like language barriers, physical barriers, or attitudinal barriers. By removing these barriers, teachers can ensure that all students have equal access to the curriculum and the resources they need to be successful. This can include providing students with accommodation or modifications tailored to their needs.

Inclusive teaching and learning are essential for creating an equitable learning environment where all students succeed. It is vital to build a school community that is welcoming to everyone, regardless of their background, beliefs, or abilities. By embracing this concept, educational institutions can create a learning environment that is more inclusive and diverse.

In an inclusive classroom, teachers need to think about the diversity of their students and how they can make their teaching methods more accessible to them. This may involve accommodations for different learning styles, providing resources in multiple languages, or using technology to reach learners uniquely. Teachers also need to be aware of their unconscious biases and ensure that their teaching practices are not perpetuating any existing inequalities.

Creating an equitable learning environment requires teachers to go beyond traditional teaching methods and be mindful of the diversity of their students. They should consider any potential learning styles and provide resources in multiple languages. Technology can be used to reach learners in unique ways, providing them with the necessary tools to grow and develop.

Importantly, teachers must be aware of any unconscious biases that may be present in the classroom and ensure that their teaching practices do not perpetuate any existing inequalities. For example, they should take special care to avoid discrimination based on gender, race, ethnicity, or any other characteristic. By creating an inclusive learning environment that is welcoming to everyone, educational institutions can foster a sense of belonging among all learners.

Educational institutions have the power to create a more equitable learning environment and break down existing inequalities. To do this, they must be aware of the needs of all learners and create a safe and welcoming environment for everyone. This means avoiding any form of discrimination, whether it is based on gender, race, ethnicity, or any other characteristic.

Educational institutions can proactively create an inclusive learning environment by fostering a sense of belonging. This can be accomplished by providing adequate resources and support for all students, regardless of their background. Educators should also be aware of and sensitive to their biases and be willing to challenge their assumptions to create an equitable learning environment.

Ultimately, it is the responsibility of educational institutions to create an inclusive learning environment where all students can thrive. By doing this, they can ensure everyone can access a quality educational experience and help create an equitable educational system.

3.1 Designing an Inclusive Curriculum

The term 'inclusive curriculum' refers to a teaching approach encompassing the diversity of students' backgrounds, abilities, and learning styles. An inclusive curriculum aims to create a learning environment that accommodates all students and ensures that all students receive the support they need to succeed. It's important to recognize that all students have different needs and that teachers must consider this in their teaching approach.

An inclusive curriculum is an approach to teaching that looks at the overall learning environment, from the classroom elements to the materials and activities offered. It considers the diversity of students' backgrounds, abilities, and experiences and works to create an environment that supports their individual learning needs. This could include accommodating different learning styles, providing extra support for those who need it, and creating an atmosphere where all students feel safe and respected.

The objective is to ensure that all students have an equal opportunity to explore and learn in a way that is meaningful to them. This means that teachers should be flexible in their teaching styles, adapting their strategies to suit the individual needs of their students. It also means recognizing the importance of collaboration and building relationships with students to ensure that their learning needs are met. Finally, it is essential to be aware of potential barriers in the classroom, such as language, culture, or race, and to be prepared to address these to create an inclusive learning environment.

In designing an inclusive curriculum, teachers must be aware of the various learning styles of their students and create an environment that encourages their growth and development. This can be achieved by incorporating activities that appeal to different learning styles. It's also essential to create a curriculum that is culturally sensitive and responsive to the needs of all students. This can be accomplished by creating activities that reflect the cultures and backgrounds of the students in the classroom.

Educators should strive to create a conducive learning environment for all students. To do this, they should understand their students' different learning styles and design activities that engage and challenge them. Additionally, teachers can create a curriculum that includes various cultures and backgrounds by incorporating exercises that reflect the diversity of their student body. This can be achieved by engaging students in activities that are meaningful to them and that honor their unique backgrounds and experiences.

It is also essential to be aware of potential barriers that may exist in the classroom, such as language, culture, or race. By understanding how these barriers impact learning, teachers can create strategies and interventions to address them. This can include providing resources or support for students struggling with language or cultural differences to ensure their needs are met. Ultimately, by creating an inclusive learning environment, teachers can ensure all students can access the same educational opportunities.

Creating a safe and inclusive space for learning starts with creating an environment that encourages collaboration and communication. This means encouraging open dialogue between students and teachers and providing opportunities for students to work together and participate in activities that will help them develop problem-solving and critical-thinking skills.

These activities should be tailored to the individual needs of each student, taking into account any language and cultural differences that may exist. These activities should also be adapted to meet the different learning styles that students may have so that all students have access to the same educational opportunities. It is also essential to provide resources and support for students who struggle with language or cultural barriers to meet their needs.

Lastly, teachers should create an environment that promotes collaboration and communication. This can be done by encouraging open dialogue between students and teachers and providing opportunities for students to work together and participate in activities promoting problem-solving and critical thinking. By doing this, teachers can create a safe and inclusive space for learning.

3.2 Incorporating Inclusive Pedagogical Practices

Incorporating inclusive pedagogical practices in the teaching process not only helps to create a safe and respectful learning environment for all, but it also allows diversity and its potential to be fully acknowledged and explored. This means creating learning experiences that recognize the unique needs of individuals and create opportunities for everyone to achieve their academic potential.

Creating an inclusive environment for learning is key to allowing students the opportunity to reach their full potential. This environment should be one where all students are respected and their voices heard. All students should be encouraged to participate and engage in class discussions and activities regardless of their cultural and linguistic backgrounds. By providing a safe space for all students to engage in the learning process, teachers can create an environment where students feel comfortable expressing their ideas and experiences and feel valued as individuals.

In addition to creating an inclusive environment, teachers should also use pedagogical practices that recognize the unique needs of each student. This could include using different methods of instruction, such as visuals, games, and activities, as well as adapting materials to each student's individual learning style. It is also important to provide students with resources to support their learning, such as providing access to books, technology, and other materials. By taking these steps, teachers can ensure that all students have the resources they need to reach their academic potential.

In order to do this, instructors need to understand the diverse cultural, economic, and linguistic backgrounds of their students. This begins with developing an awareness of how these backgrounds influence the way students learn and how they interact with each other. Additionally, instructors should be aware of systemic inequalities and how these can create barriers to learning. They should also be aware of the various forms of discrimination that may be present in the classroom and actively work to prevent them.

It is essential for instructors to understand how their students learn in order to provide the best possible education. Factors such as cultural, economic, and linguistic backgrounds can influence the way students learn and interact with each other. Instructors should also be aware of systemic inequalities and actively work to address these issues. This can include taking action to prevent discrimination in the classroom, such as calling out problematic language, monitoring student interactions, and providing a safe space for all students.

Additionally, instructors should provide resources to support their students' learning. This may include providing access to books, technology, and other materials, as well as tailoring instruction to each student's individual learning style. By providing these resources, teachers can ensure that all students have access to the tools they need to reach their academic potential. Taking these steps can be instrumental in creating an inclusive learning environment in which all students can thrive.

Incorporating inclusive pedagogical practices also requires that instructors provide differentiated instruction and assessment, which takes into account the learning styles and preferences of their students. This can include providing a variety of instructional materials and engaging in activities that are designed to meet the needs of all students. Additionally, it involves assessing student learning in ways that are meaningful and appropriate to the student's ability.

Differentiated instruction and assessment can be a powerful way to ensure that all students receive an education that meets their individual needs. For example, teachers can provide visual, auditory, and tactile materials to students, allowing them to access information in ways that are best suited to their strengths. Similarly, teachers can use a variety of assessment methods to evaluate what students have learned, such as oral presentations, written assignments, and peer-review activities.

By engaging in these practices, teachers can create an inclusive learning environment conducive to the development of all students. This can include providing additional resources to students who may need extra support, fostering collaboration among students, and tailoring instruction to each student's individual learning style. By providing these resources, teachers can ensure that all students have access to the tools they need to reach their academic potential. Taking these steps is instrumental in creating an inclusive learning environment in which all students can thrive.

3.3 Addressing Power Dynamics in the Classroom

The power dynamics between teachers and students are essential to the education environment. When teachers know how different power dynamics affect their classrooms, they can ensure that students are treated equally and respectfully. This includes understanding teachers' and students' roles within the school and how those roles can shape the learning environment.

When teachers know the power dynamics in their classroom, they can create an environment where all students are respected and treated equitably. This includes understanding teachers' and students' roles within the school and how those roles can affect the learning experience. For example, teachers act as authority figures and facilitators of knowledge, while students are expected to participate in their learning actively. If teachers are aware of these roles, they can lead by example and provide students with the tools they need to be successful.

In addition, teachers should also be aware of any power imbalances that exist between themselves and their students. This could come in the form of age, gender, or socioeconomic status, for example. Teachers must understand and acknowledge these power dynamics to ensure that all students receive the same respect and support. By recognizing these dynamics, teachers can create a safe and equitable learning environment where all students can thrive.

Teachers can use various strategies to address power dynamics in the classroom. These can include fostering an equitable learning environment where students are free to ask questions, encouraging open and honest dialogue, and using a variety of teaching styles to ensure that all students are included. Teachers can also create an atmosphere of respect, where all opinions are valued, and each student is respected for their experience.

Power imbalances in the classroom can be pervasive, and these dynamics can harm students. Teachers must recognize and acknowledge these power dynamics to ensure that all students receive a fair and equitable learning experience. The best way to do this is to create an atmosphere of respect and open dialogue in the classroom, while also accommodating a variety of learning styles to suit the needs of all students. Additionally, teachers should encourage students to ask questions and create an environment where all opinions are respected and valued, regardless of socioeconomic status. Doing so ensures that all students feel safe and empowered to express themselves in the classroom.

By taking the time to understand and address power dynamics in the classroom, teachers can create an equitable learning environment that allows all students to thrive. This can be done by fostering meaningful dialogue, providing different teaching styles, and creating an atmosphere of respect in the classroom. Ultimately, acknowledging power dynamics can help teachers create an environment where students feel heard, valued, and respected, regardless of their socioeconomic status.

A teacher's primary responsibility is to create a classroom environment that allows all students to thrive. This means providing instruction, fostering meaningful dialogue, accommodating different teaching styles, and creating an atmosphere of respect. Embracing power dynamics is an integral part of this process.

It is vital for teachers to recognize and acknowledge the power dynamics between themselves and their students and to ensure that these dynamics are not used to the detriment of any student. This includes being conscious of any power imbalances in the classroom - such as gender, race, or socioeconomic status - and creating an environment where all students feel heard, respected, and valued.

By understanding the power dynamics in the classroom, teachers can create an equitable learning environment for all students. This can be accomplished by encouraging student participation, ensuring everyone is heard, and creating a safe space for students to express their opinions. Ultimately, taking the time to understand and acknowledge the power dynamics in the classroom can help teachers create a more equitable and inclusive learning environment.

Finally, teachers need to recognize the power dynamics between themselves and their students and to take steps to ensure that those dynamics are not used to the detriment of any student. This includes being aware of any power imbalances in the classroom, such as gender or race, and working to create an environment where all students feel safe, respected, and valued. By understanding the power dynamics in the classroom, teachers can create an equitable learning environment for all students.

CHAPTER FOUR

4.0 Recruiting and Retaining Diverse Faculty and Staff

When it comes to recruiting and retaining diverse faculty and staff, colleges and universities must take a proactive approach. Diversity initiatives should be integrated into the hiring process, which includes outreach to potential candidates from all backgrounds. This can be done in a number of ways, such as attending job fairs and networking events, utilizing online job boards, and partnering with organizations that specialize in connecting employers with diverse job candidates.

Creating a diverse faculty and staff is an essential part of creating an inclusive and equitable campus environment. Institutions of higher education must be intentional in their recruitment and retention efforts to ensure that they are reaching out to potential candidates from all backgrounds.

One way to do this is to incorporate diversity initiatives into the hiring process. This could include attending job fairs and networking events specifically geared towards diverse candidates, utilizing online job boards that specialize in connecting employers with diverse job seekers, and partnering with organizations dedicated to connecting employers with diverse job candidates. Additionally, universities should strive to create an inclusive and welcoming environment through their communication materials, website, job postings, and other recruitment materials.

These efforts are essential for universities to ensure that their faculty and staff reflect the diverse student body they serve and the communities of which they are a part. Ultimately, when universities can foster an inclusive and equitable campus environment, they will be better equipped to provide an education that is truly accessible to all.

It is also important to create a supportive and respectful environment for diverse faculty and staff once they are hired. This includes providing an equitable workplace and offering professional development opportunities that recognize and celebrate different cultures and backgrounds. Furthermore, it is essential to ensure that diverse faculty and staff have access to the same resources and opportunities as their colleagues. This includes access to research funding, mentorship programs, and other career-advancement initiatives.

Having a diverse faculty and staff is not enough for universities to foster an inclusive and equitable campus environment. It is important to provide a supportive and respectful environment for these diverse faculty and staff members. To do this, universities should strive to create an equitable workplace, where everyone is treated fairly and given equal opportunities.

Professional development opportunities should also be offered that recognize and celebrate different cultures and backgrounds. This can help to educate the campus community about diversity and inclusion and allow faculty and staff to learn from one another. It is also essential to ensure that diverse faculty and staff have access to the same resources and opportunities as their colleagues. This includes research funding, mentorship programs, and other career-advancement initiatives. By providing these resources and initiatives, universities can create an environment where everyone can thrive and succeed.

To create an equitable and inclusive atmosphere, higher education institutions need to go beyond simply recruiting diverse faculty and staff. It is also essential to ensure that all faculty and staff are given the same resources and opportunities regardless of their background. This includes providing research funding, mentorship programs, and other career-advancement initiatives.

These resources and initiatives should be designed to provide all employees with the same chances to succeed and progress in their careers. For example, an effective mentorship program could provide support and guidance to all staff, allowing them to gain valuable skills and knowledge regardless of their background. Similarly, research funding could provide a financial safety net for all faculty to pursue their academic interests.

By taking a proactive approach to creating a more equitable and inclusive atmosphere, institutions of higher learning can provide a positive working environment for all their faculty and staff. With the right resources and initiatives in place, everyone can have the chance to thrive and succeed.

4.1 Enhancing Hiring Practices

Regarding hiring practices, organizations increasingly focus on diversity, equity, and inclusion (DEI). Implementing DEI hiring practices involves more than simply increasing the number of diverse candidates. It requires a company to ensure that they are actively creating an equitable recruitment process and culture that considers the needs of all applicants.

Organizations committed to DEI hiring practices must ensure that they create an environment in which everyone is treated fairly and equally. This involves more than just looking at and considering the qualifications of all applicants. It also requires considering how the recruitment process and company culture might impact different candidates.

For example, a company might be committed to increasing the number of people from underrepresented backgrounds hired. However, if the recruitment process is not accessible to all potential candidates or if the company culture does not foster inclusion and respect for all employees, then this goal will not be achieved. Companies must work to create a recruitment process and culture that is equitable and inclusive for everyone.

The goal of DEI hiring practices is to create an equitable and inclusive workplace. Companies should ensure their DEI initiatives are rooted in a comprehensive plan prioritizing diversity, equity, and inclusion. This plan should be reviewed and updated as necessary to accommodate changes in the workplace over time.

Creating an equitable and inclusive workplace starts with the recruitment process. Companies should ensure their recruitment process is accessible to all potential candidates. It should be designed to provide a level playing field for all types of candidates. For example, the recruitment process should not favor candidates from specific backgrounds or degrees.

Once candidates are hired, companies should also work to ensure that the workplace culture fosters inclusion and respect for all employees. This means creating an environment where people from different backgrounds are accepted and respected, and all employees feel safe and valued. Companies should consider developing policies that promote diversity and inclusion, such as anti-discrimination policies. They should also train employees on cultural sensitivity and appropriate workplace behavior.

By following these steps, companies will be better positioned to create an equitable and inclusive workplace for everyone. This is essential for achieving the goal of DEI hiring practices.

Organizations should also take steps to ensure that their recruitment processes are free from any bias. This includes designing interview processes that are structured in a way that allows candidates to showcase their skills and qualifications. Companies should also consider introducing measures that help assess candidates' soft skills and cultural fit for the company. Additionally, organizations should look for ways to reduce bias during hiring by using blind resumes or other tools.

To ensure that recruitment processes are fair and bias-free, organizations should consider using blind resumes. This means that candidate names and other identifiers are removed from resumes, making it easier for employers to assess the skills and qualifications of the candidate through a more objective lens. Additionally, organizations should consider introducing assessment tools to help evaluate a candidate's soft skills and cultural fit within the company. This could include personality tests or assessments of communication and problem-solving skills.

It is also essential for companies to create an equitable and inclusive workplace culture. This could involve introducing anti-discrimination policies and providing employees with training on cultural sensitivity and appropriate workplace behavior. This kind of training should be provided for all staff, from new hires to senior management. By taking these steps, organizations can create an environment where everyone feels respected and valued. This is a crucial step in achieving the goal of diversifying their hiring practices.

4.2 Advancing Diversity in Leadership Roles

Organizations need to foster an environment of inclusivity to attract and retain talented individuals from diverse backgrounds. Companies that commit to diversity in their leadership roles are more likely to be successful. A diverse group of leaders will bring a range of ideas, experiences, and perspectives to the table, helping to create a better work environment and inspiring innovation in the workplace.

Diversity can be a powerful tool for organizations looking to get ahead. Having a varied set of people from different backgrounds in leadership roles can help to create an atmosphere of acceptance and understanding. This environment can help attract and retain talented individuals who can bring unique perspectives and ideas to the table.

A diverse group of leaders can also help inspire workplace innovation. Different perspectives can lead to better problem-solving and more creative solutions. This can be especially beneficial in a competitive market where businesses must stay ahead of the curve. A diverse group of thinkers can help ensure that the organization is always one step ahead of the competition.

In addition to the potential for increased innovation and creativity, a diverse group of leaders can provide valuable insight into different markets. Having leaders from different backgrounds can help to give a better understanding of how to reach and engage with customers from diverse backgrounds. This can be a powerful tool for organizations looking to expand their customer base and increase their profits.

Having a diverse leadership team is more than just an opportunity for employees to succeed. It is also a way to create a more inclusive and supportive work environment. People from different backgrounds, experiences, and perspectives can offer new ideas and solutions that may not have been considered. This can help organizations stay ahead of the competition and ensure their products and services are the best they can be.

Furthermore, having a diverse leadership team can bring insight into different markets. Leaders from different backgrounds can provide valuable insight into how to reach and engage with customers from different backgrounds. This can be a powerful tool for organizations looking to expand their customer base and increase their profits. Moreover, leaders from diverse backgrounds can help to create a more culturally aware company, allowing for a better understanding of the diverse needs and wants of customers from different cultures.

Recruiting and providing resources to individuals from different backgrounds can help organizations create a more diverse leadership team. This is essential for companies that want to remain competitive in today's global market. Offering training and mentorship programs to those from various cultures and backgrounds will allow them to learn the skills and knowledge they need to become successful leaders. It will also provide a platform for these individuals to share their unique perspectives and experiences with the company.

Organizations should also focus on creating an inclusive environment that encourages the growth of all individuals. This includes providing them with the necessary resources to help them reach their goals and foster a sense of belonging. Companies should strive to create a space where everyone feels respected and valued, regardless of their background or culture. Doing so will help make a more culturally aware company, allowing for a better understanding of customers' different needs and wants from different cultures.

To promote diversity in leadership roles, organizations must create an inclusive environment that values the unique skills of all individuals. To do this, companies should focus on recruiting diverse candidates and providing opportunities for them to grow. They should also provide training and mentorship programs for individuals from diverse backgrounds and resources to help them develop the necessary skills and knowledge to become successful leaders. This will help ensure that everyone in the organization has the chance to reach their full potential.

4.3 Supporting Professional Development

Professional development is a vital aspect of an individual's career, and employers are increasingly recognizing this. Workers need to stay abreast of developments and trends in their field to remain competitive. Employers can help their employees by supporting professional development through tuition reimbursement, paid training opportunities, and skills-building resources.

Employers increasingly understand the importance of investing in their employees' professional development. Providing support for professional development helps to ensure that their employees remain competitive and up to date with the latest knowledge and trends in their field. This support can come in tuition reimbursement for furthering education, paid training opportunities, or skills-building resources.

These resources can help employees stay ahead of the curve in their industry and gain the skills necessary for career advancement. For example, tuition reimbursement can enable employees to attend college courses or seminars to acquire the latest knowledge and skills. Paid training opportunities can also help employees stay abreast of the latest trends and best practices in their area. In addition, employers can provide skills-building resources, such as access to online learning platforms or mentorship programs.

Employers may want to consider tuition reimbursement to motivate employees to further their professional development. This incentive allows employees to pursue courses and certifications related to their jobs without worrying about the financial burden of tuition. Additionally, employers can provide additional funds for conferences and seminars so their employees can stay current on the latest developments and trends in their field.

Not only does tuition reimbursement allow employees to gain the latest knowledge and skills in their field, but it also encourages them to invest in their career growth. Employees who take advantage of tuition reimbursement will be better equipped to handle their current job duties and be better prepared for future opportunities. Furthermore, employers can provide access to online learning platforms and mentorship programs to further enhance employee skill-building.

Paid training can also be an excellent way for employers to support professional development. Employers can provide employees access to online courses, webinars, and other learning opportunities. They may also give employees the time and resources to attend in-person conferences and seminars. This can help employees stay current on trends and developments in their field while still being able to perform their job duties.

Providing employees with the resources to build their skills is an excellent way for employers to ensure they have a well-trained staff. Employers can give access to online courses, webinars, and other learning opportunities to help their employees stay updated on trends and developments in their field. Books, articles, and other materials can also be provided to employees to help them build their knowledge and expertise.

Additionally, employers can provide their employees with the time and resources to attend in-person conferences and seminars. This can help employees stay abreast of the latest trends while still being able to perform their job duties. Employers can also create career development opportunities by offering mentoring and internship programs. These programs can help employees build their skills and gain valuable experience.

Finally, employers can provide resources for their employees to build their skills. This can include access to online courses, books, or other materials to help employees develop their knowledge. Employers may also offer in-house training with respect to trending opportunities.

Part II: Fostering an Inclusive Campus Climate

CHAPTER FIVE

5.0 Cultivating Intercultural Competence

Cultivating intercultural competence is a way of understanding different cultures and being equipped to interact with them confidently and comfortably. It involves getting to know the culture's customs, norms, values, and expectations and identifying cultural differences. To cultivate intercultural competence, being open-minded, respectful of different cultures, and willing to explore and learn from them is essential.

Intercultural competence is not just a matter of simply understanding different cultures but also being able to bridge the gap between them. One must actively engage in cultural exchange and reflection to cultivate intercultural competence. Immersing oneself in the culture and being open to the experiences and perspectives of others can help foster understanding and break down cultural barriers.

It is also essential to recognize that different cultures may have different communication styles. For example, some cultures are more direct, and others are more indirect. Recognizing and adjusting to these differences can help create a sense of understanding and respect. Additionally, it is essential to remember that everyone has unique life experiences and perspectives, which can often be rooted in their culture. Listening to and understanding these perspectives can help build trust and create better relationships.

It also involves building skills such as communication, empathy, and self-awareness, essential for successful intercultural interactions. Communication should be tailored to a specific culture, considering the culture's language, body language, and customs. Empathy is also essential, as it helps to create meaningful connections and understanding between people from different cultures. Lastly, self-awareness helps to identify one's cultural assumptions and biases, allowing for more effective communication.

When engaging in intercultural interactions, it is essential to have an open mindset and be willing to learn about different cultures. Taking the time to understand and appreciate the differences between cultures can go a long way in ensuring the conversation is thriving. Building communication, empathy, and self-awareness skills can make intercultural interactions more accessible and meaningful.

Communication is vital in cross-cultural communication, as it should be tailored to the specific culture. This includes considering the culture's language, body language, and customs. Additionally, having empathy for the person from the other culture can help build meaningful connections and understanding. Lastly, self-awareness is necessary to identify cultural assumptions and biases, allowing for more effective communication.

Understanding the importance of cultural differences is crucial for fostering respectful and safe intercultural interactions. Taking the time to learn about different cultures can help develop a sense of understanding and respect. Additionally, it is essential to remember that everyone has unique life experiences and perspectives, often rooted in their culture. Listening to and understanding these perspectives can help build trust and foster better relationships.

Cultivating intercultural competence makes it possible to create successful interactions and relationships between people of different cultures. This can lead to increased respect and understanding and more productive and meaningful conversations. Ultimately, this can help create a more harmonious and inclusive society where people of different backgrounds can co-exist peacefully.

Learning about different cultures can provide meaningful insight into the lives of others. It can help us better understand their beliefs, values, and customs, which are often rooted in their cultures. With this knowledge, it is possible to create successful interactions and relationships between people of different cultural backgrounds. By building bridges of understanding, respect, and trust can be fostered.

In addition to understanding the cultural backgrounds of others, it is essential to remember that everyone has unique life experiences and perspectives. Listening to and understanding these different perspectives can help build stronger relationships with others. It can also lead to more productive and meaningful conversations.

Ultimately, cultivating intercultural competence makes it possible to create a more harmonious and inclusive society where people of different backgrounds can co-exist peacefully. This can lead to greater appreciation and acceptance of diversity, which can benefit all individuals.

5.1 Understanding Cultures and Identities

Cultures and identities are the unique characteristics and qualities that define a person or group. Understanding and appreciating these qualities can help to foster a sense of belonging and inclusion. Understanding the cultures and identities of those around us is essential to creating a positive community where we can all thrive.

Cultures and identities are the foundation of who we are as individuals and as a collective. They provide us with a sense of security, purpose, and pride. They give us a sense of belonging, a connection to our past, and a way to create a shared future.

We must learn to appreciate and understand the cultures and identities of those around us to foster an inclusive and positive community. This involves understanding the nuances of different cultures and identities and recognizing how we are all connected. It is essential to be open to new perspectives and learn from one another to create a safe and prosperous environment.

We can cultivate a sense of belonging and inclusion through education, dialogue, and shared experiences. We must strive to create an environment where everyone is respected, valued, and supported. This can be achieved through understanding our identities and cultures and those of our friends, family, and peers. We can create a harmonious and inclusive community only when we deeply understand our own and others' cultures and identities.

Cultures can be based on shared values, beliefs, norms, and language. These values shape how individuals interact with each other and the world around them. It is essential to recognize the cultural perspectives of others to create a sense of understanding and respect. Furthermore, it is necessary to acknowledge and celebrate the diversity of cultures in our communities.

Creating a sense of understanding and respect is paramount for fostering a harmonious and inclusive community. To achieve this, individuals must gain a deep understanding of their own culture and identity, as well as the cultures and identities of their family, friends, and peers. Doing so makes it possible to recognize the shared values, beliefs, norms, and language that define a culture. This can be achieved through open dialogue, education, and celebration of the diversity that exists in our community.

Moreover, when we recognize and appreciate the cultural perspectives of others, it fosters a sense of respect and appreciation - thereby creating an environment in which people feel respected, valued, and supported. This is especially important in a globalized world where people with different cultural backgrounds interact daily. By understanding and respecting the cultures of others, it is possible to create an environment where people feel connected and accepted.

Identities can be based on gender, age, race, religion, ability, and sexual orientation. It is essential to understand and respect the identities of those around us and not make assumptions about individuals based on their individuality. Creating an inclusive environment requires understanding and recognizing the rights and needs of all individuals, and creating an environment where everyone feels safe and valued.

In today's globalized world, understanding and respecting the identities of those around us is more important than ever. This means understanding individuals' different backgrounds, histories, and experiences and being aware of the impact of our words and actions on them. It is essential to create an environment where everyone feels respected, valued, and supported, regardless of their identity.

This is especially true regarding the rights and needs of those belonging to minority groups. It is essential not to make assumptions about individuals based on their identity, such as gender, age, race, religion, ability, or sexual orientation. Providing a safe and inclusive environment requires understanding these identities and creating an environment where everyone feels accepted and safe. This can be achicved through open dialogue and mutual respect.

5.2 Developing Intercultural Skills

Intercultural skills are becoming increasingly critical in today's globalized workplace. To succeed in an international business environment, it is necessary to have a good understanding of different cultures and backgrounds. This is particularly important in a global or multicultural setting, as it allows people to work together in harmony and respect.

By developing intercultural skills, people can learn how to navigate cultural differences respectfully and professionally. This helps create a positive atmosphere where all parties understand each other and can work together effectively. Additionally, intercultural skills can be beneficial for those looking for a job in a multicultural environment, as employers often look for people who can interact with people from different backgrounds.

Developing intercultural skills is becoming increasingly important in today's globalized world. By understanding different cultures and backgrounds and navigating cultural differences, one can be successful in a global or multicultural setting. Intercultural skills also benefit those looking for a job in a multicultural environment.

Intercultural skills are essential for anyone in today's interconnected and ever-changing world. By understanding different cultures, navigating cultural differences, and developing empathy, active listening, and open-mindedness, individuals can be better prepared for success in a global or multicultural setting. This is particularly true for those looking for jobs in a multicultural environment.

Formal training programs, such as courses offered by universities or language schools, can help develop these skills. Everyday experiences, like talking to people from different cultures and learning about various customs and beliefs, can also help. Learning a foreign language can be particularly useful, as it can foster a better understanding of other cultures. Moreover, participating in international exchange programs can provide invaluable insight into different cultures and help individuals gain the intercultural skills they need.

Intercultural skills are essential for success in today's world. They can help foster better relationships with colleagues, clients, and customers and open up new opportunities for career advancement and growth. With the right combination of knowledge, practice, and experience, anyone can develop the intercultural skills needed for success.

Gaining intercultural skills is not always easy; however, the effort is worth it. Building relationships across cultures requires a willingness to learn and understand different customs and beliefs. While studying cultural norms can be helpful, actively engaging in other cultures is often essential. Participating in activities such as attending cultural events, going on cultural exchange trips, and participating in international programs can be highly beneficial.

Learning a foreign language is also a great way to gain intercultural skills. Not only can it help bridge cultural gaps, but it can also foster a deeper understanding of different cultures. Being able to communicate in a foreign language can give individuals a richer experience of other cultures and enhance their intercultural skills. Additionally, participating in international exchange programs can provide invaluable insight and help individuals gain the intercultural skills they need. These programs offer an excellent opportunity for individuals to experience different cultures firsthand and build strong relationships with people from other countries.

Foreign language learning is an essential part of intercultural skills. It not only helps with communication, but it can also give individuals a deeper understanding of different cultures. This understanding can come in many forms, such as talking to people in their native language, understanding the customs and beliefs of another culture, and understanding cultural perspectives.

Developing intercultural skills can also involve participating in cultural events and activities. Attending cultural events, such as festivals, can provide insight into different cultures and be a great way to connect with people from various backgrounds. Additionally, engaging in cultural exchange trips, like studying abroad, can be an enriching experience. Not only does it offer an opportunity to learn about different cultures, but it also helps individuals build relationships with people from diverse backgrounds. Participating in international programs is also an excellent way to gain intercultural skills. These programs provide individuals with a deeper understanding of other cultures and the skills necessary to succeed in a foreign environment.

5.3 Encouraging Dialogue and Engagement across Differences

When engaging with someone with different opinions, it is vital to remain open-minded and respectful. Our preconceived beliefs and assumptions can get in the way of understanding the other person's point of view. We should strive to create a safe and comfortable dialogue and meaningful exchange space.

It is also essential to recognize that dialogue across differences can be difficult and uncomfortable. We may not have all the answers and may even be confronted with ideas we disagree with. It is okay to be wrong and to make mistakes. We should be open to new perspectives and learn from each other.

Dialogue across differences is an excellent opportunity for growth and understanding. By having meaningful conversations, we can increase our empathy and develop relationships with others. This can help us become more informed and better understand different cultures, experiences, and perspectives.

To encourage dialogue across differences, it is essential to practice active listening. This means listening to someone else's perspective completely without interruption or judgment. It is also necessary to avoid making assumptions about someone's beliefs and experiences; instead, ask questions if you are unsure. It is critical to be open to learning from someone else and understanding why they think and feel the way they do.

Listening to someone else's perspective without interruption or judgment is essential for meaningful group dialogue. This active listening allows us to avoid assumptions about someone's beliefs and experiences. If we are unfamiliar with a person's story, we must ask questions to gain insight and understanding. Being open to learning from others helps to create an environment of respect and appreciation.

By engaging in meaningful conversations, we can increase our empathy and develop relationships with others. This can help us understand different cultures, experiences, and perspectives. Rather than dismissing someone else's point of view, we should strive to see the world through new lenses. This can help us to expand our worldview and gain a better understanding of our global community.

In addition, it is critical to be respectful when engaging with someone different from you. Respectful dialogue requires speaking calmly and politely. It also means not attacking someone's beliefs or experiences and instead working together to find common ground. Finally, being aware of your biases and privileges is essential. Acknowledging these can be a powerful way to open dialogue across differences.

Respecting someone different from you is essential for meaningful dialogue. We should begin by speaking kindly and not making assumptions about someone's beliefs or opinions. We should also take the time to listen and understand another's point of view, rather than trying to make ourselves heard. In this way, we can form a connection and find common ground.

We must also be aware of the biases and privileges that come with our unique backgrounds. We must be conscious of our rights to recognize the differences of others. Acknowledging these differences can not only open a dialogue between us, but it can also help us to understand the world around us better.

Finally, it is essential to understand different cultures, experiences, and perspectives. This will allow us to gain knowledge that would otherwise be inaccessible. Seeing the world with a new perspective can help us expand our worldview and better understand our global community.

CHAPTER SIX

6.0 Building Inclusive Student Support Services

When it comes to student support services, having an inclusive approach is paramount. The goal is to create a safe and welcoming environment for all students, regardless of their gender identity, race, ethnicity, disability, or any other factor. To achieve this, universities and colleges should ensure their services are accessible.

Creating an inclusive environment can be a challenge, mainly because the needs of students vary greatly. Recognizing that students may have different backgrounds and experiences that can affect their academic success is essential. For example, a student who is a member of a historically marginalized group may need extra support to overcome the challenges they face in the classroom.

Universities and colleges should strive to provide services tailored to each student's needs. This includes offering resources tailored to their needs, such as mental health services for those struggling with anxiety or depression. Universities and colleges should also support students who may not feel comfortable in the traditional classroom setting. This can include providing online courses or offering alternative learning spaces to allow students to work in a more relaxed environment.

One way to make support services more inclusive is to provide various resources. This could include offering counseling services, providing information about financial aid and scholarship opportunities, and creating peer support groups. Creating an environment that is culturally sensitive and respectful of a student's needs is also essential.

Students' mental health is an important issue, and universities and colleges should provide support for those who may suffer from anxiety or depression. Such resources may include counseling services, which can help students cope with their mental health issues in a safe and confidential environment. Additionally, information regarding financial aid and scholarship opportunities should be provided to ensure that students can pursue their educational goals despite any mental or financial obstacles.

Peer support groups can also be beneficial, as they allow students to share their stories and experiences. Furthermore, universities should strive to create an environment that respects each student's unique needs and cultural background. This could involve providing alternative learning spaces for those who may not feel comfortable in a traditional classroom setting. Online courses could also be offered to allow students to learn in an environment more conducive to their individual needs.

Schools should also strive to create an inclusive learning environment that meets the needs of all students, regardless of their disability. This can include providing adaptive technology and resources to ensure students with disabilities can access the same education as their peers. By creating a learning environment that is welcoming and accessible to all, universities and colleges can ensure that all students have an equal opportunity to succeed.

Providing resources to students with disabilities can be a way for schools to create an inclusive learning environment. This could include offering accessible textbooks, providing assistive technology such as text-to-speech software, and having staff trained in adaptive technology. Additionally, schools could provide additional support services such as tutoring or mentoring programs to ensure that all students have the opportunity to reach their educational goals.

Creating a welcoming and inclusive learning environment is essential for all students, regardless of their unique needs and cultural backgrounds. This could involve providing alternative learning spaces for those who may not feel comfortable in a traditional classroom setting. Online courses could also be offered to allow students to learn in an environment more conducive to their individual needs. Such measures can help ensure that all students have an equal opportunity to access the same quality of education and succeed in their studies.

Furthermore, universities and colleges should be proactive in recognizing and responding to the needs of students based on their unique needs and cultural backgrounds. For example, they can provide specialized tutoring services, additional support networks, or alternative learning spaces for those who may not feel comfortable in a traditional classroom setting. Additionally, schools should consider offering online courses for students who may feel more comfortable learning in an environment tailored to their needs. By creating an environment that is welcoming and inclusive to all, universities and colleges can help ensure that all students have access to the same quality of education.

6.1 Providing Culturally Responsive Services

Providing Culturally Responsive Services Culturally responsive services require a deep understanding of the cultures of the populations they serve. This includes an understanding of the cultural values, beliefs, and practices of the population, their language, and other aspects of their cultural experience. It also requires an understanding of how cultural differences can create barriers to accessing services and how to provide services in ways that are respectful of the population's culture.

Services that are culturally responsive recognize the diversity of the populations they serve and strive to meet their needs. They take into account the cultural differences among individuals and aim to create a safe and welcoming environment for everyone. This includes providing language interpreters, ensuring that staff is culturally competent, and offering services in ways that are respectful of different cultures.

Culturally responsive services strive to create an environment in which individuals from diverse backgrounds feel comfortable and respected. This includes recognizing the importance of religion, respecting cultural practices, and ensuring that everyone is treated with dignity and respect. Additionally, it is important to ensure that services are provided in a way that is meaningful to the population being served. This includes taking into account the individual's language, cultural values, and other cultural considerations.

Organizations providing culturally responsive services ensure that the community they serve is respected and valued. This means taking into account the cultural differences between individuals and striving to create a safe and welcoming environment for everyone. To do this, organizations provide services that demonstrate a commitment to understanding the community they serve. This includes offering language interpreters, providing staff that are culturally competent, and offering services in ways that are respectful of diverse cultures.

By recognizing the importance of religion, cultural practices, and providing services in a way that is meaningful and respectful to the population being served, organizations are ensuring that individuals from diverse backgrounds feel comfortable and respected. This includes taking into account an individual's language, cultural values, and other cultural considerations. To ensure that these services are effective, organizations must understand the needs of the community and strive to meet them in a meaningful and respectful way.

Culturally responsive services require practitioners to be aware of their own cultural values and biases, recognizing how these can influence interactions with clients. Practitioners must also be conscious of the ways in which their own cultural values can influence their perception and evaluation of the people they serve. They must be willing to challenge their own cultural beliefs and values when they conflict with the cultural values of the population they are serving.

Providing culturally responsive services requires practitioners to be self-aware and to check their own biases. They must take into account the language, cultural values, and other cultural considerations of the population they are serving. This means being open to understanding and accepting the different cultural values of the individuals they work with. Practitioners must also be willing to question and challenge their own cultural beliefs and values to better understand the communities they serve.

It is important for practitioners to take the time to understand the unique needs of the community they are serving. This includes researching the cultural backgrounds of the individuals they are working with and understanding their perspectives and experiences. Practitioners must also be open to learning about the different cultural values, languages, and other cultural aspects of the individuals they serve. By doing so, organizations can ensure that their services are tailored to meet the specific needs of the community.

Culturally responsive services also require practitioners to be knowledgeable about the historical and current context in which their clients live and the impact of this on their lives. This includes understanding the effects of racism and other forms of discrimination and the ways in which these have impacted the populations they serve. Practitioners must be willing to use this knowledge to modify their interventions to meet the needs of the population they are serving.

Working with diverse cultures requires practitioners to have an open mind and a willingness to learn. Practitioners must be willing to listen to the needs of their clients and put themselves in their shoes. This requires an understanding of the various social influences that have shaped their lives, such as racism and discrimination. Having this knowledge allows practitioners to modify their interventions to best meet the needs of the population.

Moreover, practitioners should also be aware of the different cultural values, language, and other cultural aspects of the individuals they serve. This can help organizations ensure that their services are tailored to their clients' unique needs. Doing so requires practitioners to build a positive rapport with their clients, so they can understand their perspectives and experiences.

By taking a culturally responsive approach, practitioners can provide better quality services and support to their clients. This can help improve the quality of life for people from all backgrounds, and ensure that they are treated with respect and dignity.

Culturally responsive services are tailored to the language, culture, values, and beliefs of the individual or community receiving them. This approach has been shown to improve outcomes for clients, as it helps reduce barriers that can arise when services don't consider culture. To provide culturally responsive services, it's essential to understand the culture of the target audience and to be aware of any potential biases or assumptions that might arise.

Culturally responsive services are an important part of providing quality care and support for people from different backgrounds. This approach takes into consideration the language, culture, values, and beliefs of the individual or community being served. With this approach, practitioners can better understand the perspectives and experiences of the people they are serving and can provide better quality services.

Research has shown that by taking a culturally responsive approach, practitioners can reduce the barriers that can exist when services are not tailored to the needs of the individual or community. This can result in improved outcomes and a higher quality of life for people from all backgrounds. Additionally, this approach also helps to ensure that people are treated with respect and dignity, regardless of their culture or background.

It is also important to ensure that the services being offered are appropriate for the population in question. This includes understanding the needs of the population, as well as the resources that are available to meet those needs. Additionally, the staff providing the services should be trained in how to be culturally sensitive and aware of any potential cultural issues that may arise.

Customized and culturally appropriate services are essential for providing effective health care. By taking into account the cultural background of individuals and communities, health care providers can ensure that their services are not only effective but also respectful. This includes understanding the needs of the population and the resources available to meet those needs. Additionally, staff should be trained to recognize any potential cultural issues that might arise. Such cultural sensitivity and awareness can help ensure that the services provided are tailored to the specific population in question.

By offering services that are tailored to the individual and their community, healthcare providers can help ensure improved outcomes and a higher quality of life for everyone. This approach also ensures that people are treated with dignity, regardless of their cultural background. By recognizing and respecting the differences between cultures, healthcare providers can build trust and foster stronger relationships with individuals and communities, ultimately leading to more positive health outcomes.

Acknowledging the importance of cultural sensitivity in healthcare is crucial, as it can lead to improved outcomes for patients. Health providers need to be aware of the cultural needs and values of the population they serve. To achieve this, they should strive to understand the beliefs, practices, and values of the community. They should also strive to develop services that are tailored to the specific needs of the community.

Healthcare providers should also look for feedback from the community they serve to ensure that their services are effective and appropriate. They should be open to making changes if the feedback suggests that their services are not meeting the needs of the community. Finally, healthcare providers should strive to provide services that are culturally responsive and tailored to the needs of the community. By doing so, they can foster trust and create a more positive environment for providing quality healthcare.

Finally, it is important to be open to feedback from the community and to be willing to make adjustments as needed to ensure that the services being offered are effective and appropriate for the target population. By taking these steps, we can provide culturally responsive services that are tailored to the needs of the community and are effective in achieving desired outcomes.

6.2 Supporting Underrepresented Student Populations

When it comes to supporting underrepresented student populations, higher education institutions are responsible for creating an inclusive learning environment. This includes assisting those who may need additional resources and support to succeed in their education. This could consist of providing targeted help for students from historically underrepresented communities in higher education.

Higher education institutions must foster an equitable learning experience for all students. This includes offering support for those who require extra resources to help them succeed, such as those from minority backgrounds. This support can come in the form of access to specialized courses and programs, which can provide a more comprehensive understanding of topics. It can also include targeted resources geared specifically toward underrepresented student groups, such as financial aid, mentorship, and career counseling.

These resources can help to create a level playing field in the classroom, allowing all students to participate and benefit from the educational opportunities. Furthermore, by offering targeted resources to minority students, higher education institutions are helping to improve the prospect of an equitable future for all students. By providing the necessary support, these institutions can help reduce the disparities between different student populations and create a more inclusive learning environment.

Institutions can seek to provide support services for students who need guidance and resources to navigate the college experience. This could include offering mentoring opportunities to help students gain the skills and resources they need to find success. Additionally, institutions should look for ways to increase access to financial aid and scholarships for all students, especially those from underrepresented communities. This could include creating scholarship and grant opportunities for students from specific backgrounds.

By providing support services and access to financial aid and scholarships, higher education institutions are putting forth an effort to make college more accessible and achievable for all students. Mentoring opportunities allow students to learn the skills they need to succeed while providing a support system they can turn to for guidance. Meanwhile, scholarships and grants can help reduce the financial burden and offer opportunities to students who may have had fewer resources.

Additionally, institutions can offer support and guidance to help students navigate the college experience. This could include providing resources to help students better understand college requirements and expectations and offering support services to help students in need of guidance and assistance. Through these efforts, institutions can work to reduce the disparities between different student populations and create a more equitable and inclusive learning environment.

Higher education institutions are essential in promoting equity and inclusion on campus. They can do this by providing resources to help students understand college requirements and expectations better. This could include offering information sessions, workshops, and other helpful services to give students the guidance they need. Additionally, institutions should look to provide support services to those students who may need additional assistance. This could range from providing mental health resources to offering academic advising and tutoring.

The goal of these efforts should be to reduce the disparities between student populations and create a more equitable and inclusive learning environment. To this end, institutions should look for ways to foster a culture of inclusion on campus. This could include developing programming and initiatives to celebrate diversity and create an environment of acceptance and understanding. These efforts can help create an environment that is supportive of all students, which can help underrepresented populations feel more at ease and supported in their academic pursuits.

Finally, institutions should look for ways to foster a culture of inclusion on campus. This could include developing programming and initiatives to celebrate diversity and create an environment of acceptance and understanding. These efforts can help create an environment that is supportive of all students, which can help underrepresented populations feel more at ease and supported in their academic pursuits.

6.3 Promoting Mental Health and Well-being

Mental health and well-being are among the most critical components of a successful, functioning workplace. Creating an environment that promotes these values is essential for businesses to thrive. Diversity, Equity, and Inclusion (DEI) provides a unique opportunity to make sure all employees feel seen, heard, and respected.

DEI initiatives are an important part of creating a healthy and inclusive workplace. Not only do they ensure that everyone is given an equal opportunity to succeed, but they also help to eliminate any unconscious biases that may exist in the workplace. By fostering an environment that includes everyone, regardless of background, businesses can create a welcoming and supportive atmosphere.

Furthermore, DEI initiatives can help to reduce the stress and anxiety that can arise in the workplace and help to create a space where employees feel safe to express themselves. DEI encourages open dialogue and communication, which can help to create a more harmonious work environment. Additionally, it can help to ensure that all employees feel respected, appreciated, and valued for their unique perspectives and contributions. Ultimately, DEI initiatives are essential for creating a workplace that is both mentally and physically healthy.

When DEI (Diversity, Equity, and Inclusion) is implemented thoughtfully, it can lead to improved mental health and overall well-being. Companies should ensure that everyone in the workplace is able to share their unique perspective and be an active participant in the organization. This means that all employees should feel equipped to voice their opinions without fear of judgment or exclusion.

DEI initiatives provide a platform for dialogue and communication that can help to foster an atmosphere of understanding and respect. This can create a more open and harmonious work environment where employees from all backgrounds can come together to collaborate, share ideas, and work towards a common goal. Furthermore, by actively listening to each other and engaging in meaningful conversations, all employees can feel respected, appreciated, and valued for their unique perspectives and contributions.

An effective DEI initiative should also be focused on creating a safe and healthy workplace, both mentally and physically. This means providing access to resources such as mental health support, social activities, and other wellness benefits. By creating an environment that promotes physical and mental well-being, companies can ensure that their employees remain productive, motivated, and engaged.

Ultimately, DEI initiatives are essential for creating a workplace that is both inclusive and supportive.

In addition, companies should strive to create meaningful conversations around mental health. This could involve setting aside time for employees to discuss their experiences with mental health and to provide support to each other. Organizations should also strive to provide wellness benefits, such as flexible work schedules or health reimbursement programs, to ensure that employees have access to the resources they need to stay mentally and physically healthy. By promoting mental health and well-being through DEI, businesses can create a more inclusive, supportive workplace.

Creating conversations around mental health is a crucial step for organizations to provide employees with the support they need. These conversations should provide employees with the opportunity to share their experiences and should be conducted in a safe and supportive environment. Additionally, businesses should seek to provide their employees with resources to support their mental health, such as access to mental health professionals, social activities, and other wellness benefits.

By offering these resources, companies can show their employees that they are invested in their well-being. This will help create a more inclusive and supportive work environment, one in which employees feel safe to express themselves and be their true selves. Furthermore, taking proactive steps to create a healthy work environment can help ensure that employees remain productive, motivated, and engaged. Ultimately, DEI initiatives are essential for creating a workplace that is both inclusive and supportive.

Creating an environment that supports employees' mental health is essential for a successful business. Opening up conversations in a safe and supportive atmosphere gives employees the opportunity to share their experiences, which helps build a sense of trust and understanding. Moreover, providing resources such as access to mental health professionals, social activities, and wellness benefits shows employees that their well-being is a priority for the company.

These initiatives will also create a more inclusive and supportive workplace. By offering a safe space for employees to express themselves and be their true selves, businesses will foster a culture of respect and understanding. Additionally, taking proactive steps to promote employees' mental health can help ensure that they stay productive, motivated, and engaged. Ultimately, DEI initiatives are key for creating a workplace that is both inclusive and supportive.

CHAPTER SEVEN

7.0 Promoting Equity and Access in Higher Education

Promoting equity and access to higher education ensures everyone has an equal opportunity to pursue a college degree regardless of their background, ethnicity, or gender. This includes providing resources and support services to students who are underrepresented in higher education, such as first-generation college students or those from low-income households. Additionally, it is essential to ensure that all students have access to a quality education that meets their needs and provides them with the skills and knowledge necessary to succeed in the workforce.

Promoting equity and access to higher education promises a more equitable society. It means everyone has the same opportunity to pursue a college degree regardless of background, ethnicity, or gender. This can be achieved through the implementation of policies that are designed to level the playing field. For example, providing resources and support services to historically underrepresented students in higher education can help reduce the educational disparities that have been present in the past.

Additionally, ensuring that all students are provided with a quality education that meets their needs and gives them the skills and knowledge to pursue their desired career path is essential. This could involve the introduction of relevant courses and programs that are tailored to the specific needs of the student. It is also necessary to allow students to engage in extracurricular activities that will enable them to develop and refine their skills outside of the classroom. Finally, offering financial aid and scholarships can help make college more affordable for those from lower-income households.

Promoting equity and access to higher education is critical for expanding student opportunities. Institutions of higher learning must create an environment where all individuals feel comfortable and have equal opportunities to prosper. This can include providing low-cost transportation, affordable housing, and food assistance. Furthermore, universities and colleges should offer various support services for students, such as academic advisors and career counselors.

Equitable access to higher education is essential to create a level playing field for all students. Institutions of higher learning must foster a culture of inclusivity where everyone feels safe and supported. They should provide resources such as low-cost public transportation, affordable housing, and food assistance to ensure that no one is excluded from the opportunity to pursue higher education.

In addition, universities should have adequate support services in place for students, such as academic advisors, career counselors, mental health services, and other resources that cater to students' individual needs. It is also essential to offer students the opportunity to engage in extracurricular activities to help them develop their skills and knowledge outside the classroom. Furthermore, providing financial aid and scholarships can help make college more affordable for those from lower-income households.

This can be accomplished through various initiatives, such as providing financial aid to needy students, creating mentorship programs to help students adjust to college life, or expanding enrollment to underserved populations. Additionally, universities and colleges can work to create a more diverse and inclusive campus environment where all students feel welcome and valued. This includes providing resources and support for students from historically marginalized backgrounds and promoting culturally responsive teaching and learning in the classroom. Finally, universities and colleges can work to create pathways for students to enter into a variety of career fields so that they can be successful in the workplace.

Creating pathways for students to enter various career fields is an invaluable part of the college experience. From helping students create resumes and apply for internships to providing mentorship and networking opportunities, universities and colleges can provide the necessary resources and support for students to be successful in the workplace.

In addition, universities and colleges must create a more diverse and inclusive campus environment that values all students. This can include providing resources and support for students from historically marginalized backgrounds and promoting culturally responsive teaching and learning in the classroom. Furthermore, expanding enrollment to underserved populations is critical to creating a more equitable college experience.

Finally, providing financial aid to students in need and creating mentorship programs to help them adjust to college life can help make college more accessible and affordable. This can also allow students to engage in extracurricular activities, which can help them develop their skills and knowledge outside of the classroom.

7.1 Financial Aid and Scholarships

DEI Financial Aid and Scholarships are an excellent way for students to fund their education. With various options available, students can apply for federal and private assistance. Federal assistance includes grants, loans, and work-study programs. Confidential assistance includes scholarships, grants, and loans from private organizations and institutions.

Finding financial aid to fund a college education can be daunting. Thankfully, there are many options to help alleviate the financial burden. Students should be aware of both federal and private assistance.

Federal assistance includes grants, loans, and work-study programs. Grants are awarded based on financial need and do not have to be paid back. Loans are also available to students and must be paid back with interest. Work-study programs allow students to work part-time and earn money to help pay for college expenses.

Private assistance is provided by organizations and institutions outside of the federal government. This includes scholarships, grants, and loans. Scholarships are awarded based on various criteria, such as academic excellence, talent, and volunteering. Grants are typically awarded for a specific purpose, such as research or study abroad. Private loans are available but usually have more stringent requirements than the federal government, such as a credit check and a co-signer.

Grants are a popular form of financial aid for students to help pay for college. They are typically awarded based on various criteria, such as academic excellence, talent, and volunteering. Grants are provided by the government, universities, and other organizations and are typically awarded for a specific purpose, such as research or study abroad.

Private loans are also an option for students to pay for college but typically have more stringent requirements than the federal government, such as a credit check and a co-signer. Banks, credit unions, and other financial institutions offer private loans, which are usually more expensive than federal loans. However, they can cover expenses not covered by other aid sources, such as living expenses.

The first step in applying for financial aid is to fill out the Free Application for Federal Student Aid (FAFSA). This form is available online and should be completed as soon as possible. Once completed, the FAFSA will be sent to the appropriate federal and state agencies to determine a student's eligibility for financial aid. Depending on the student's circumstances, they may qualify for grants, loans, work-study, or a combination of these options.

The Free Application for Federal Student Aid (FAFSA) is essential for students and families seeking higher education. The form can be completed online and should be submitted as soon as possible. After submitting the FAFSA, it will be sent to the appropriate federal and state agencies to determine a student's eligibility for financial aid.

Students may qualify for grants, loans, and work-study programs depending on their financial situation. Grants are funds given to students that do not have to be repaid. These funds can help cover tuition, fees, and other educational expenses. Loans must be repaid with interest, usually after a student has graduated. With work-study programs, students can earn money through part-time jobs on campus. Scholarships are also available from private organizations and institutions. These awards are typically merit-based and may or may not need to be repaid. Although these awards may not cover the entire cost of tuition, they can go a long way in helping a student pursuc higher education.

Scholarships are an attractive source of funding for college students. Several types of scholarships are available, from federal and state grants to university-specific awards. These awards are often merit-based and can be used to cover tuition or other educational expenses.

DEI Financial Aid and Scholarships provide an excellent way for students to fund their education. Most schools have a financial aid office that can assist students in finding scholarships for which they may be eligible. Additionally, many private organizations and institutions offer scholarships to students. These awards are typically merit-based and may or may not need to be repaid. Although these awards may not cover the entire cost of tuition, they can go a long way in helping a student pursue higher education.

Research is vital when it comes to scholarships. Students should take the time to explore their options and determine what type of financial assistance they qualify for. There are a variety of websites that offer scholarship search tools to help students find the right program for their needs. Additionally, students should contact the financial aid office at their school for more information.

7.2 Addressing Accessibility and Accommodations

Ensuring equitable access to an organization's resources and activities is essential for creating a space where everyone can thrive. Providing accessibility and accommodations for those in the diverse and inclusive community (DEI) is a significant part of this. To create an accessible environment, organizations should consider physical, communication, and technological accommodations.

Physical accommodations involve changing the physical environment to make it easier for those with disabilities or other needs to access and participate in activities. This may include ramps, elevators, widened doorways, and accessible seating. Additionally, organizations should consider making their spaces and activities accessible to all by providing tactile signage, Braille signage, and large print materials.

Communication accommodations ensure everyone can participate in activities and share their thoughts and ideas. This can involve providing interpreters, captioning, or other communication assistance for people with hearing impairments. It is also essential to create an inclusive environment by using language that is respectful and free from bias or assumptions.

Organizations should first assess the physical and environmental conditions of their space. Are the pathways clear, or are there obstacles that could impede access for those with disabilities? Are there enough accessible restrooms and seating areas? Are there places where people can go to take a break from sensory overload? Ensuring the environment is accessible is essential for creating a safe and welcoming space.

Creating an accessible environment goes beyond just providing physical accommodations. Organizations should also consider ensuring everyone can participate in activities and share their thoughts and ideas. This may involve providing interpreters, captioning, or other communication assistance for individuals with hearing impairments. It is also essential to foster an inclusive environment by using language that is respectful and free from bias or assumptions.

For example, organizations should ensure that their documents and other materials use gender-neutral or gender-inclusive language. They should also use person-first language, such as "person with a disability" instead of "disabled person." This shows respect for the individual and acknowledges their humanity. In addition, organizations should strive to create a space where everyone is respected regardless of race, religion, gender identity, or sexual orientation. By taking these steps, organizations can create an environment of inclusion and acceptance for all.

Organizations should go beyond simply providing resources and strive to create an environment where everyone feels safe and accepted. This means building a culture of embracing diversity, and DEI community members feel respected. For example, this can include using people-first language when referring to someone in the DEI community, such as saying "a person with a disability" instead of "a disabled.

Organizations should also put policies in place that protect members of the DEI community from discrimination. This includes ensuring that employees receive proper training on respecting and interacting with those in the DEI community. It also involves creating a safe and secure environment for all employees, regardless of race, religion, gender identity, or sexual orientation. Finally, organizations should provide resources for those in the DEI community to access and use. These could include access to counseling services, job training programs, and other resources.

Creating a safe and secure environment for all employees is essential for any organization. This means providing an environment that is inclusive and free of discrimination based on race, religion, gender identity, or sexual orientation. Companies should strive to create a workspace free of prejudice and promote mutual respect and understanding.

In addition, organizations need to provide resources for those in the DEI community. This could include access to counseling services, job training programs, and other resources that help these individuals thrive. It is also essential to ensure that these resources are accessible and available to all.

Furthermore, it is necessary to provide a platform for members of the DEI community to connect and support one another. This could include setting up mentorship programs or networking opportunities.

Finally, organizations should consider technological accommodations to ensure everyone can access their resources. This may include providing assistive technology, such as screen readers, and ensuring that any websites or digital resources are accessible to those with disabilities. Additionally, organizations should consider providing training opportunities for those needing additional assistance with navigating technology.

7.3 Closing the Opportunity Gap

The Opportunity Gap refers to the disparity between people of color and white people in terms of access to opportunities. This gap can be seen in various areas, including education, employment, and housing. Diversity, Equity, and Inclusion (DEI) initiatives are designed to address this gap and provide equitable access to opportunities for everyone.

DEI initiatives are a way to bridge the Opportunity Gap. They focus on ensuring that people of color have the same access to education, employment, and housing opportunities as white individuals. To achieve this goal, DEI initiatives often involve providing resources and support, such as mentorship programs and career development workshops, to people of color. Additionally, DEI initiatives may include policy changes and legislative reforms to ensure everyone has equitable access to opportunities.

DEI initiatives are also designed to create a culture of inclusion and respect. This can include strategies such as increasing diversity in the workplace, introducing cultural competency training, and creating an environment where all people feel valued and respected. By fostering an inclusive culture, DEI initiatives help ensure that people of color are not subject to discrimination in the workplace or other areas of life. Ultimately, DEI initiatives strive to provide everyone with the same opportunities and access to resources, regardless of race or ethnicity.

DEI initiatives require intentional effort to ensure everyone is treated fairly and has the same opportunities. This means focusing on the representation of people of color in leadership roles, providing training to ensure everyone has equal resources, and creating an inclusive workplace culture that fosters respect and acceptance. Organizations should also strive to close the opportunity gap by providing access to education, employment, and housing opportunities available to everyone.

Developing and fostering an inclusive culture is critical to the success of DEI initiatives. This includes ensuring that people of color are not subject to discrimination in the workplace or other areas of life. Organizations should strive to create a safe and supportive environment that values diversity and encourages people to speak up and express their ideas without fear of judgment. This can be achieved by providing a platform for open dialogue and fostering a culture of respect and acceptance. Additionally, organizations should ensure everyone has the same opportunities and access to resources regardless of race or ethnicity.

DEI initiatives involve creating policies and structures that increase opportunities for specific groups. This includes increasing the representation of people of color in leadership positions and providing training and support to ensure everyone has access to the same resources. DEI initiatives also focus on creating an inclusive workplace culture where everyone feels welcome and respected. By offering these resources, organizations can close the opportunity gap and ensure equal access to education, employment, and housing opportunities.

Diversity, Equity, and Inclusion (DEI) initiatives are becoming increasingly important for organizations and employers. These initiatives go beyond just preventing discrimination in the workplace; they also seek to create an environment where everyone is treated with respect and given access to the same resources. To achieve this, organizations must work to ensure that people of color are represented in leadership roles and that diversity is embraced in the workplace.

Organizations should also strive to provide training that ensures everyone has access to the same resources and is given the same opportunities. This could include providing access to education, employment, and housing opportunities and closing any existing pay gaps. Finally, organizations should work to create an inclusive culture where all employees are respected and accepted and any biases or microaggressions are addressed. By creating an inclusive culture, organizations can ensure everyone is treated fairly and has the same opportunities.

Part III: Navigating Challenges and Embracing Opportunities

CHAPTER EIGHT

8.0 Intergroup Dialogue and Conflict Resolution

Intergroup Dialogue and Conflict Resolution utilizing DEI is an effective and impactful way to address complex and tangled issues between groups. This approach is based on a unique combination of Dialogic Education and Intergroup Dialogue. It enables individuals to explore their biases, prejudices, and values in an atmosphere of mutual respect. In addition, DEI allows for exploring various perspectives and, ultimately, resolving conflicts. With this approach, people can better understand themselves and their respective groups while also learning to collaborate and build bridges between communities. This approach is especially beneficial for communities that have experienced trauma and are historically marginalized. DEI can help build trust between groups and create a safe environment for open dialogue. This approach can open the door to mutual understanding and increased collaboration when conducted respectfully and effectively.

DEI (Dialogic Education and Intergroup Dialogue) is a powerful tool for conflict resolution between different groups. It helps people recognize and examine their prejudices, biases, and values in a respectful environment. DEI enables individuals to understand other viewpoints and constructively resolve conflicts. The approach is beneficial for communities facing trauma or those that have been historically oppressed.

DEI can help build trust between different groups, providing a safe platform for constructive dialogue. It is the chance to listen to and learn from one another while working together to build bridges and mutual understanding. Through this approach, individuals can develop empathy and compassion for each other and work together to create meaningful solutions. This type of dialogue helps to break down barriers and create an inclusive environment where everyone is treated with respect and dignity. By engaging in DEI, individuals can better understand themselves, their respective groups, and the wider community.

DEI also promotes collaboration and understanding between groups by creating a safe environment for difficult conversations. Through this approach, participants can respectfully share their perspectives and experiences and create a space where all individuals feel heard and respected. This type of dialogue helps to foster understanding between communities and to create an atmosphere of mutual respect and understanding. DEI can also help break down the barriers between groups and develop a sense of unity and understanding.

Diversity, Equity, and Inclusion (DEI) is essential in today's workplace. It is a holistic approach to creating an environment that is respectful and inclusive of all individuals. Through DEI, organizations can create an atmosphere of understanding, collaboration, and respect while promoting meaningful dialogue among those from different backgrounds and experiences.

By creating a safe space for difficult conversations, DEI encourages individuals to respectfully share their perspectives and experiences. This type of dialogue is essential in creating an atmosphere of mutual respect and understanding between different communities. DEI also helps break down the barriers between groups and foster a sense of unity and understanding. Additionally, DEI can help to create a workplace where everyone feels included and respected, regardless of their background.

By implementing DEI, organizations can create a safe and inclusive environment. By engaging in meaningful dialogue and creating an atmosphere of understanding, DEI can help to foster collaboration and understanding between different groups. This type of dialogue can help to create an environment of mutual respect and performance while also helping to break down barriers and create an inclusive environment for all.

Ultimately, the DEI practice helps create a more equitable and inclusive environment where all individuals are treated with respect and understanding. Through this practice, individuals learn to recognize and appreciate different perspectives and to work together to create a more inclusive community. DEI is an invaluable tool for building understanding and collaboration between individuals and groups and promoting mutual respect and understanding.

DEI involves engaging in meaningful dialogue between individuals and groups to foster understanding and collaboration. It is a practice that encourages individuals to recognize and appreciate the perspectives and experiences of others, and it works to break down barriers and create an inclusive environment for all. It can create an atmosphere of mutual respect and understanding and help build bridges between different groups.

Through DEI, individuals are empowered to create an equitable and inclusive environment where all individuals are treated with respect and dignity. This practice encourages people to listen to each other, understand their differing perspectives, and work together to create a more inclusive and harmonious community. DEI provides a valuable tool for building understanding and collaboration between individuals and groups and encouraging mutual respect and understanding.

The practice of Intergroup Dialogue and Conflict Resolution utilizing DEI (Diversity, Equity, and Inclusion) is a powerful tool for creating understanding and dialogue between people of different backgrounds, experiences, and beliefs. This practice encourages participants to engage in meaningful dialogue and to recognize and address the power dynamics within the group. Participants learn to work together to identify common goals and to find solutions that promote understanding and respect for all individuals and groups in the conversation.

DEI focuses on understanding and addressing the unique needs of each individual within the group and understanding the impact of different perspectives on the group as a whole. It promotes open communication, active listening, and respect for all participants. Through this process, participants learn to recognize and appreciate the diversity of experiences and perspectives within the group and to use this knowledge to address conflicts constructively and respectfully. The result is a more inclusive and equitable group dynamic where everyone is treated with respect and understanding.

Participants in DEI practice learn to communicate openly and actively listen to one another. They are encouraged to share their experiences and beliefs in a safe and respectful environment. This promotes meaningful dialogue and helps participants recognize and address power dynamics within the group. Through this process, they can better identify common goals and find solutions that honor all individuals and groups in the conversation.

DEI also emphasizes the importance of understanding and addressing each person's unique needs in the group. By recognizing the group's diversity of experiences, perspectives, and beliefs, participants can work together to create a more equitable and inclusive atmosphere. This helps foster understanding and respect for everyone involved in the conversation, promoting collaboration and problem-solving. Participating in DEI practice can create a more inclusive and equitable group dynamic.

8.1 Facilitating Dialogues on Controversial Issues

When facilitating dialogues on controversial issues, it is essential to ensure that everyone is heard and their perspectives are considered. A DEI lens provides a framework for understanding and validating the views of all involved. It is essential to use empathy to ensure conversations are conducted in a way that is respectful, productive, and inclusive.

To effectively use a DEI lens, it is essential to understand the perspectives of all participants. This includes actively listening to the stories and experiences of others and taking the time to reflect on how they may be different from our own. It also means respecting the rights and opinions of all involved and ensuring that no one is silenced or discriminated against.

Using a DEI lens can help to create a safe and inclusive environment where everyone feels heard and respected. It also helps to ensure that conversations are productive and meaningful and that reaching an understanding is as equitable as possible. Ultimately, a DEI lens can help ensure that all perspectives are considered and that dialogues on controversial issues are conducted in a respectful, productive, and inclusive way.

Implementing a DEI lens into a conversation regarding a controversial issue is essential to understanding the perspectives of each participant involved. This means allowing each person to provide their own opinion or point of view and listening to them intently. It is also essential to be mindful of any biases or preconceived notions, as they can prevent any meaningful dialogue from occurring.

Additionally, it is vital to use empathy when having these conversations. Validate the other person's opinion and feelings about the issue, no matter how different it may be from your own. Understanding and respecting the other person's view will foster a more productive and inclusive environment. This will enable everyone to engage in meaningful dialogue that can provide solutions to complex issues.

Using a DEI lens for conversations regarding controversial issues is a great way to ensure that all perspectives are considered and that the dialogue is conducted respectfully and inclusively.

To effectively utilize a DEI lens when facilitating dialogues on controversial issues, one must approach the conversation with an open mind and understand how different people can have different experiences and opinions. Recognizing and accepting the validity of different perspectives is essential, even if one disagrees. Being able to do this requires the skill of empathy, which can be practiced and developed.

An essential part of using a DEI lens when facilitating conversations regarding controversial issues is to create an environment of understanding and respect. This means that everyone should be encouraged to express their opinions in a way that is respectful of each other. This can be done by allowing a safe space to share ideas without judgment or criticism. Additionally, it is essential to actively listen to one another and acknowledge the other person's opinion and feelings about the issue, no matter how different it may be from your own.

It is also essential to intentionally create a space that includes everyone's perspectives. This means ensuring that everyone is represented in the conversation and that all views are considered. This can be done by actively seeking diverse opinions and ensuring everyone is heard. Doing this will help foster meaningful dialogue, and solutions to complex issues can be explored. Ultimately, using a DEI lens for conversations regarding controversial topics is a great way to ensure that all perspectives are considered and that the dialogue is conducted respectfully and inclusively.

Using DEI lenses for conversations about controversial issues can be a beneficial tool for fostering dialogue between individuals with different views and experiences. It encourages people to come together in a respectful and safe space, allowing them to express their thoughts without fear of judgment. People can share their opinions and experiences while being mindful of each other's feelings and perspectives. This encourages constructive dialogue and allows for a more productive and meaningful conversation.

The DEI lenses allow all parties involved to have an equal chance to be heard and understood and heard without criticism or interruption. It also provides a safe environment for discussing complex and potentially sensitive issues. People can work together to find solutions to these issues by using empathy and understanding. This way, meaningful dialogue can occur, and solutions to complex problems can be explored, ensuring that all perspectives are considered. Ultimately, using a DEI lens for conversations regarding controversial topics is a great way to provide respectful and inclusive dialogue.

8.2 Addressing Conflict and Promoting Restorative Practices

Conflict is an inevitable part of life, especially in the workplace. But when it is addressed in a timely and effective manner, it can be used as an opportunity to build understanding, empathy, and trust. Restorative practices provide an effective way to address workplace conflict. It is an approach that seeks to repair relationships and hold those responsible accountable for their actions. Restorative practices promote a culture of inclusivity by fostering an atmosphere of respect and mutual understanding.

Restorative practices involve a range of strategies designed to address workplace conflict and build a culture of inclusivity. These strategies include dialogue, mediation, and restorative circles, all of which focus on addressing the root causes of conflict and repairing relationships. In a dialogue, parties involved in the conflict are encouraged to talk openly about their feelings and perspectives. Mediation involves a neutral third-party facilitating the conversation to help parties reach a resolution. Restorative circles involve a group of people coming together to share their perspectives and collectively brainstorm solutions.

The goal of restorative practices is to promote healing and understanding between those involved in the conflict and ultimately create a more harmonious work environment. This is done through open and honest communication, which encourages employees to be vulnerable and express their authentic feelings. Additionally, restorative practices provide an opportunity for those involved to learn from their mistakes and develop a deeper understanding of each other's perspectives, ultimately leading to increased trust and respect. Restorative practices are beneficial to both employees and employers, as they allow for the resolution of conflicts in a timely and effective manner, while also fostering a culture of inclusivity and understanding.

Utilizing restorative practices, all parties involved in a conflict are given the opportunity to be heard and understood. This can help build understanding and empathy by giving everyone a chance to express their feelings and perspectives. Additionally, this can help create a stronger sense of community and connection among all members of the workplace.

Restorative practices have the potential to create a more dynamic and productive workplace environment. By allowing for meaningful dialogue between those in conflict, it can create a space for growth and understanding. This can be especially beneficial for employers, as it allows them to identify and address issues quickly and proactively. Additionally, it can create a sense of openness and understanding between employers and employees, which in turn can lead to increased trust and respect.

The key to successful restorative practices is to ensure that all parties involved feel heard and respected. This means that everyone should be given the chance to express their feelings and perspectives. It also means that everyone should be given the chance to develop a deeper understanding of each other's points of view. Furthermore, this type of dialogue can help to foster a sense of community and connection among all members of the workplace. Ultimately, this can lead to improved morale, productivity, and well-being in the workplace.

Dialogue is an important part of creating a supportive and inclusive environment. It allows individuals involved to share their perspectives and feelings and to have a chance to explain their reasoning. Through dialogue, all participants can learn more about each other and develop a deeper understanding of each other's points of view.

For restorative practices to be effective, it is important to create a safe and supportive space for dialogue. This means providing clear expectations and guidelines and utilizing active listening to ensure that all participants feel heard. Additionally, it is important to foster collaboration and compromise, as well as an atmosphere of respect that encourages all members of the workplace to work together to resolve conflicts. Ultimately, this can lead to improved morale, productivity, and well-being in the workplace.

Creating a safe and supportive space for dialogue is essential for restorative practices to be successful. It is important to be clear about expectations and provide guidelines for the conversation. Additionally, it is necessary to use active listening to make sure that all parties feel heard.

Furthermore, fostering collaboration and compromise is key to resolving workplace conflicts. Respect should be demonstrated between all members of the workplace so that they can work together to find a resolution. This can lead to increased morale, productivity, and well-being. Inclusive environments are beneficial for all involved as they have the chance to express their perspectives and feelings. Through dialogue, everyone can learn more about each other and develop a deeper understanding.

CHAPTER NINE

9.0 Engaging Allies and Building Alliances

Building meaningful relationships with allies is not just necessary for creating a strong DEI alliance, but it is also essential for sustaining it. When people come together in collaboration, they build trust and understanding between each other. This trust and compassion can increase visibility and a greater sense of belonging.

A strong DEI alliance also allows multiple groups to come together and work towards a unified goal. This unified goal can be anything from a shared mission statement to a collective effort to support marginalized communities. These groups can create a safe and welcoming environment for all members through collaboration. This environment can foster empathy and understanding between different groups, which can help create a more diverse and inclusive environment.

Connecting with other organizations and individuals committed to advancing DEI initiatives to build a more equitable and sustainable future is essential. By engaging in meaningful dialogue and collaboration, allies can learn from and support each other's efforts. Partners should be willing to listen to each other's perspectives and find common ground to move forward together.

Collaboration is critical to creating a more equitable and sustainable future. Allies should be willing to actively listen to each other's perspectives and identify common goals. These allies can then develop joint strategies to further their shared mission. This could involve working together on campaigns to promote DEI initiatives or organizing events to increase awareness and participation.

By collaborating, allies can create a safe and welcoming environment for all members, which can help to foster empathy and understanding between different groups. Allies should be open to learning from one another and actively collaborating to create a more diverse and inclusive environment. Working together, allies can be powerful agents of change and help create a future where everyone is welcomed and respected.

Allies must also be willing to acknowledge and accept when their efforts are misguided. This means understanding that sometimes progress is slow and there are often obstacles to overcome. It also requires allies to be open to feedback and criticism and to adjust their strategies when needed. When this happens, partners should strive to find a way forward that works for everyone and ensure their work is meaningful and impactful.

To foster empathy and understanding between different groups, allies should participate in conversations about DEI and work together on initiatives that promote diversity, equity, and inclusion. They should also be open to learning from each other and actively collaborate to create a more diverse and inclusive environment. This could include attending seminars, working with other organizations, or organizing events that unite diverse communities. By doing so, allies can help create a future where everyone is welcomed and respected.

By involving the community, allies can bring a more informed perspective to DEI initiatives. They can also provide valuable insights from the community's unique perspectives. This involvement can help build trust between allies and the organization, allowing for more productive collaboration. Additionally, partners can provide a platform for open dialogue and discussion, which can be used to create a more inclusive environment.

Furthermore, allies can help create a more welcoming environment by attending seminars, working with other organizations, or organizing events that unite diverse communities. These activities create a platform where people from different backgrounds can come together and exchange ideas. By doing so, allies can help create a future where everyone is welcomed and respected. Additionally, they can provide opportunities for people to learn and grow from each other, further promoting an inclusive and diverse environment.

By establishing relationships between organizations committed to creating an inclusive environment, allies can provide support and resources to those who need it. These connections can open up opportunities for learning, networking, and growth. Partners can help to create a safe and supportive environment for those from different backgrounds. This can include providing access to resources, information, and support for people to achieve their goals.

Additionally, allies can advocate for creating a more inclusive and diverse environment.

To build relationships with these organizations, it is essential to have a clear understanding of their mission and values. Allies can research organizations and attend events to understand their goals and objectives better. Partners should also be prepared to have honest and respectful conversations about their and the organization's values. This will ensure everyone involved is aligned and working towards creating a more inclusive and diverse environment.

Finally, engaging with education, advocacy, and policy-making groups can be a great way to build DEI alliances. Talking to people who are knowledgeable about the issues and are actively trying to make a difference can help create a robust network of support for your DEI initiatives. These organizations can provide resources and guidance to help ensure that your initiatives are successful. Creating a diverse and inclusive environment is a complex but essential task. To achieve this, it's important to have allies willing to work together toward a common goal. Having allies allows an organization to better understand its goals and objectives. This is especially important for DEI initiatives, as organizations need partners who can offer resources and guidance.

Allies should also be prepared to have honest and respectful conversations about their and the organization's values. This will ensure everyone involved is aligned and working towards creating a more inclusive and diverse environment. Engaging with education, advocacy, and policy-making groups can also be a great way to build DEI alliances. Talking to people who are knowledgeable about the issues and are actively trying to make a difference can help create a robust network of support for DEI initiatives. This can give organizations the resources and guidance they need to ensure their initiatives succeed.

9.1 Empowering Allies to Support Inclusion

Inclusion is a critical element of any successful business strategy. Including and respecting everyone, regardless of background, can lead to greater creativity and productivity. To ensure the success of inclusion, it is essential to empower allies to help support it. Allies are not part of the marginalized group but recognize the need for inclusion and are willing to help make it a reality.

Inclusion is a core component of any thriving business plan. Companies can benefit from higher levels of creativity and productivity by creating a workplace where everyone is respected and included regardless of their background. To ensure inclusion is successful, it is essential to empower allies who can join the cause. Partners are not from the same minority group but still recognize the importance of inclusion and are eager to help make it happen.

These allies can advocate for the marginalized, bringing attention to the issue and ensuring their voices are heard. They can also help build an atmosphere of acceptance and understanding, creating a safe environment where everyone can express themselves without fear or judgment. Furthermore, allies can help develop policies and procedures that will ensure that all employees are treated equally and that any complaints of discrimination are taken seriously and addressed promptly.

By having allies committed to the cause of inclusion, companies can ensure that everyone feels valued and respected, leading to a more productive and enjoyable workplace. It is important to remember that inclusion is a continuous effort and that allies play a vital role in ensuring it is effective.

To create an environment where everyone feels valued and respected, companies should prioritize inclusion and take steps to ensure all employees are included. Allies, who can be from any background, can help in this effort. Partners can work to eliminate microaggressions, provide mentorship and advocacy to those who feel excluded, and act as a bridge to unite different groups in understanding. In doing so, they can help foster an environment of respect and inclusivity.

Having allies who are committed to this cause is critical to making sure that inclusion is successful. Partners can actively listen to different perspectives, understanding each individual's unique needs and helping ensure that everyone is heard and respected. They can also be a source of support for those who feel discriminated against and help create a sense of belonging and safety.

Ultimately, it is important to remember that inclusion is an ongoing effort, and allies are essential to ensuring success. By having partners dedicated to making everyone feel included, companies can ensure that everyone feels respected and valued, leading to a more productive and enjoyable workplace.

Inclusion is a process that requires continuous effort and dedication to make sure everyone is respected and feels a sense of belonging. An ally is an individual who is committed to advocating for inclusivity and supporting those who face discrimination. Partners are essential to creating an environment where everyone feels safe and welcome.

Allies are pivotal in advocating for inclusivity and creating environments where everyone feels safe and welcomed. Organizations must ensure that partners have the resources to understand inclusivity and diversity better. This can include providing access to books, articles, and seminars that provide deeper insight into the various issues facing marginalized communities.

Organizations can also create a platform for allies to share their experiences and ideas on fostering a more inclusive workplace. This could include providing partners with a space to share their stories or hosting regular meetings in which partners can discuss best practices for creating an inclusive culture. By actively listening to partners, companies can ensure everyone's voice is heard and their contributions are valued.

Finally, organizations should recognize the effort and dedication of their allies. This could include providing partners access to exclusive benefits, such as professional development opportunities, or simply identifying their work in front of their peers. This will help to ensure that allies feel appreciated and valued for their efforts.

9.2 Co-Creating Inclusive Spaces with Campus Partners

Creating inclusive spaces on campus is a collaborative effort. It requires participation and support from both faculty and students, as well as from administration and other partners. These partners can include diverse student organizations, alum groups, and other campus offices. Engaging with campus partners is essential for developing a safe, welcoming, and inclusive environment. When crafting an inclusive space, it is essential to ensure that everyone has a place at the table and that their needs and perspectives are considered. It is also essential to clearly understand the goals and desired outcomes of the space and how campus partners can help achieve them. Creating a sense of belonging is an integral part of co-creating inclusive spaces. It is vital to foster understanding, acceptance, and respect. It is also essential to be mindful of the needs and perspectives of all campus community members. By engaging with campus partners, we can ensure that everyone is included, and their voices are heard.

Creating inclusive spaces on college campuses is a shared responsibility. All university community members must strive to create a safe and respectful environment. This includes administrators, faculty, staff, students, and campus partners such as student organizations, alums, and community members. Everyone must be mindful of the needs and perspectives of their peers and be willing to foster understanding and acceptance. Inclusion is incredibly challenging in places with a history of discrimination and marginalization. It is essential to consider the different backgrounds of individuals and how negative past experiences may affect how they interact in the present. To ensure that all voices are heard, it is essential to engage with campus partners to create a culture of inclusion. Collaboration between all stakeholders is necessary in creating a space of respect and safety for all campus community members.

Campus partners are essential when creating a culture of inclusion. Faculty and staff can help lead and inspire students and advocate for those facing discrimination. Student organizations are a great way to unite people and foster understanding and acceptance for all students. Community members can provide valuable resources and insight into the challenges and opportunities in the local area. They can be a great asset in helping create a safe and respectful space for everyone on campus. All stakeholders need to come together and collaborate to ensure that everyone's voice is heard. This collaboration should include faculty, staff, student organizations, and community members. Through this, a culture of inclusion can be established that celebrates diversity and provides a sense of belonging and safety for all campus community members.

Everyone must come together and invest in the effort to create an inclusive and respectful campus. Faculty, staff, student organizations, and community members should work together and listen to each other. This collaboration will help create an environment where everyone's voice is heard and all backgrounds, beliefs, and experiences are accepted and celebrated. Through this collaboration, a culture of inclusion can be fostered, helping people form meaningful connections and build a sense of belonging. This will also help create a safe and secure campus for all students, staff, and faculty, ensuring comfort and security. Ultimately, creating an inclusive campus is a continuous process of communication and collaboration that requires everyone's commitment and effort. By coming together and listening to each other, a safe and respectful environment can be established where everyone feels welcome and respected.

Once an inclusive environment is established, it is important to ensure that it is sustained and supported. Faculty and staff members can lead by example and strive to create an environment that is sensitive and respectful to all. They can provide guidance and support to students and foster an atmosphere of understanding and acceptance. Student organizations can work together to create events and activities that celebrate diversity and promote understanding. They can also provide a safe space for students to come together and share their experiences. Community members can also be a valuable resource in helping to maintain a culture of inclusion. They can provide insight into local challenges and opportunities, as well as resources that can be used to create a more inclusive environment.

Leadership is also an important factor in sustaining an inclusive campus. The administration should lead by example and prioritize the needs of all campus community members. They should ensure that everyone feels safe and respected and that their voices are heard. Faculty and staff should also strive to be role models and help create a culture of inclusion. By engaging with campus partners and investing in the effort to create an inclusive environment, everyone can work together to ensure that everyone is included and respected.

Creating and sustaining an inclusive campus is a collaborative effort. All members of the campus community, from students to faculty and staff, have a role to play in creating an environment of acceptance and respect. Students should be encouraged to participate in campus activities and initiatives and to make sure their voices are heard. Faculty and staff should also strive to be role models for inclusivity and help foster an environment of inclusion. Campus partners can also be instrumental in creating an inclusive campus. Investing resources in initiatives that promote inclusion and diversity can help ensure that all members of the campus community feel supported and respected.

Additionally, collaboration between campus partners and members of the campus community is essential to ensure that everyone's needs are met and that they are all included. By engaging with campus partners and investing in the effort to create an inclusive environment, everyone can work together to ensure that everyone is included and respected. This joint effort can help build a culture of acceptance and understanding and make sure that those who are different feel welcomed and embraced.

9.3 Allies in Advancing Diversity Initiatives

Regarding diversity initiatives, the importance of allies cannot be overstated. Allies are individuals or organizations that recognize the value of diversity and are willing to work actively to promote and support it. They are often leaders in different communities and can leverage their influence to ensure that diversity initiatives are successful. Allies can also provide unique perspectives on how best to address diversity and inclusion issues.

Allies are essential for the success of any diversity initiative. They not only have the privilege of accessing resources and networks that support such initiatives, but they also have the ability to use their influence to ensure that diversity initiatives are celebrated and respected. Moreover, they can provide unique perspectives on how to tackle the various issues surrounding diversity and inclusion. For instance, allies can share their ideas on building a fairer and more equitable workplace or ensuring that all voices are considered when designing and implementing diversity initiatives. Furthermore, allies can be invaluable in creating a safe and inclusive environment. They can challenge discriminatory behavior and language, amplify diverse voices, celebrate differences, and advocate for equal opportunities for all. They can also provide support to those who are marginalized or excluded. This support can come in many forms, such as ensuring physical and emotional safety, offering resources, or helping to build inclusion networks.

Allies can be an invaluable resource for any organization fostering an inclusive and diverse workplace. They can provide insight on how to create a more equitable workplace and ensure that all voices are heard when planning diversity initiatives. Allies can also use their experiences to support those affected by discrimination or marginalization. Furthermore, allies can motivate and inspire those around them, helping to create a sense of belonging and a safe space for those who are different. They can also use their unique positions to bridge gaps between other communities, leading to stronger relationships and a more unified environment. Finally, allies can help to promote the visibility of those who face discrimination and exclusion, providing a platform for them to share their stories and experiences and to be actively celebrated.

Allies are invaluable in creating a more inclusive environment, as they can offer a unique understanding of different communities and how to best connect with them. Partners can provide a safe platform for those excluded or marginalized to share their stories and experiences. This also helps promote visibility for those who need it and gives them a sense of belonging. Moreover, allies can offer more nuanced perspectives regarding decision-making in diverse initiatives. Their insights can help to bridge gaps between different communities, leading to stronger relationships and a more unified environment. Allies should be encouraged to contribute to the conversation, providing feedback and suggestions to ensure the initiative's goals are achievable. By doing so, partners can be crucial in driving positive change and creating a more diverse and welcoming space for all.

Having allies participate in diversity initiatives is instrumental in creating a unified environment and a more inclusive atmosphere.

Partners can provide a platform for those who face discrimination and exclusion to share their stories and experiences in a way that makes them feel seen and celebrated. Through their support and encouragement, allies can help to bring communities together and foster a sense of belonging for those who may not have a voice. In addition to promoting visibility, partners should be encouraged to contribute to the conversation in diversity initiatives. They can provide valuable feedback and ideas to ensure the initiative's goals are achievable. By doing so, allies can be essential in driving positive change and creating a stronger sense of inclusion through their support and advocacy.

Allies can be an essential part of diversity initiatives, as they can provide an outside perspective and help move the industry forward. Allies need to be informed of the goals industry and how their contributions can help achieve those goals. Allies should also be allowed to actively participate in conversations and discussions so that their ideas and feedback can be heard. Supporting allies throughout the initiative is essential in ensuring their contributions are meaningful. This support can come from providing resources and tools to help them remain actively involved in the industry.

Additionally, it is essential to recognize and thank allies for their efforts and contributions. Doing so can be a powerful way of showing appreciation and further encouraging partners to continue being involved. Having partners in diverse initiatives can help create a more equitable and inclusive environment. Through their support and advocacy, partners can be crucial in driving positive change and building a stronger sense of inclusion. This can help to ensure that diverse initiatives are successful and that everyone can benefit from them.

CHAPTER TEN

10.0 Assessing Progress and Sustaining Change

Progressing towards a goal requires an awareness of the current state of affairs. Regular assessments can provide a bird's eye view of the process, granting an understanding of what is working and what needs to be changed. It is essential to take the time to celebrate successes, as this can encourage further progress. It may be necessary to adjust the plan if it is not working as desired. This can mean making corrections to the path or the details of the plan. It can also mean that a different plan needs to be chosen entirely. Periodic assessment is the key to understanding which direction is best to take. In conclusion, progress towards goals should be tracked and assessed regularly. This can help to identify successes and areas that need improvement. Celebrating successes is essential for keeping up motivation levels, and it is necessary to make changes to the plan if it is not working. Regular assessment is the key to determining the right course of action.

Regular assessment is critical to ensure that a plan is on track and making progress towards the desired goal. It's important to be honest with yourself and take an objective look at the progress being made. This can help identify areas that are successful, as well as those not meeting expectations. For areas that aren't successful, it may be necessary to make changes to the plan. This could involve altering the approach or the timeline to achieve improvements. Conversely, it's essential to celebrate successes. Celebrating these victories can provide motivation and a sense of accomplishment, helping to keep morale high. Regular assessment and evaluation are key to determining the right course of action, ensuring that the plan is successful and the goal is reached.

Celebrating successes can be a great motivator and can help to keep morale high. Having an accountability partner can be a great asset. They can provide support and encouragement, as well as an objective opinion on any adjustments that need to be made during the process. Documenting progress and successes can make it easier to track progress and celebrate successes. This can make the goal feel more achievable and provide a sense of accomplishment. Regular assessment and evaluation of the plan is key to making sure that the goal is reached. This helps to ensure that the plan is successful, makes it easier to identify any adjustments that need to be made, and helps to stay on track. Tracking progress can also be motivating and it can be useful to set regular check-in points to stay on track.

Tracking progress is an important part of any plan for change. It allows those involved to review the progress and ensure that the plan is heading in the right direction, aiming for the desired outcome. Doing so helps make any necessary adjustments to the plan, ensuring its success. Seeing the progress made is also motivating and helps individuals stay on track. Setting regular check-in points can be useful to ensure that everything is going smoothly. Besides tracking progress, planning for how to sustain the changes made is crucial. This involves considering the resources needed to maintain the changes, such as staff or financial resources. Creating a plan for monitoring and tracking the changes over time is also essential. This ensures that the improvements are sustained and not overlooked. Furthermore, regularly reviewing the plan ensures it remains relevant and current.

Creating a plan for monitoring and tracking changes is a key factor in keeping them in place. It is essential to review the plan regularly to guarantee that it is current, and to avoid any outdated information. Furthermore, a system to receive feedback from stakeholders should be put in place. This will help to make sure that any changes that need to be made are done quickly and efficiently, and that the plan is successful. Additionally, it is important to review the progress of the plan regularly to make sure it is still suitable. This way, any necessary changes can be made and maintained to ensure the plan remains efficient.

Making a plan is an important step in achieving any goal, large or small. It's essential to have a clear outline of what needs to be done and when. This ensures that tasks are completed quickly and efficiently, making the plan successful. Additionally, it's important to review the progress of the plan regularly to ensure it remains suitable. In this way, any necessary changes can be made to maintain efficiency. It's crucial to remember that progress is not always linear.

There will be successes and setbacks along the way. Celebrating the successes and reflecting on the setbacks can help keep you motivated and focused on the end goal. In addition to tracking the plan's progress, it's also vital to review the results of each success and setback to determine what went well and what could have been improved. This insight will help in making better-informed decisions for future tasks. Staying flexible and adjusting the plan as needed is also essential. This might involve adding new tasks, removing old ones, or altering the timeline or resources required. By doing so, you can ensure that you stay on track and achieve your objectives.

Creating a system for feedback is essential to the success of a plan. This can be achieved by collecting feedback from stakeholders or other individuals and using that feedback to adjust the plan. This adjustment may involve adding or removing certain tasks, or changing the timeline or resources needed. Doing this ensures that the plan runs as smoothly as possible. It's important to understand that progress is rarely linear. There will be good days and bad days. When the plan achieves a success, it's crucial to celebrate it and reflect on the progress made. This reflection can help keep you motivated and focused on the end goal. During times of setbacks, understanding what went wrong can aid in identifying areas that require improvement. Such reflection can lead to positive changes in the plan.

Finally, it is important to create a system for any feedback received from stakeholders or other individuals. This can help ensure that necessary changes are made in a timely manner, ensuring that the plan remains as successful as possible. It's important to remember that progress is rarely linear. There will be successes and setbacks along the way. Celebrate the successes and reflect on the setbacks, as this can help keep you grounded and focused on the end goal.

10.1 Measuring Diversity, Equity, and Inclusion Goals

Measuring Diversity, Equity, and Inclusion Goals is essential for organizations to understand how their workforce is faring in diversity, equity, and inclusion. Organizations should use metrics to measure their progress in reaching their goals in these areas. This may include metrics such as the percentage of women in leadership roles, the percentage of employees from diverse backgrounds, or the rate of employee turnover. Tracking these metrics over time can help organizations identify areas of improvement and take steps to ensure their DEI initiatives are successful.

Organizations should use the data to identify areas of improvement and create tailored programs to address the disparities. For example, if the data reveals fewer women in leadership roles, the organization can create a program to provide additional mentorship and support for female employees. This program should provide training, resources, and guidance to help women reach senior positions and progress in their careers. Additionally, the data can be used to identify any barriers to entry or progression that women may face and address them accordingly.

Data can also be used to assess the performance of DEI initiatives. By tracking metrics over time, organizations can measure the impact of their DEI efforts and adjust their strategies if needed. For example, organizations can track changes in the percentage of employees from diverse backgrounds to assess their recruitment and retention strategies. Monitoring changes in employee turnover can also help organizations identify potential issues with their DEI initiatives. Ultimately, organizations should use data to evaluate the effectiveness of their DEI efforts and make any necessary changes to foster an equitable and inclusive workplace.

Employers recognize that diversity, equity, and inclusion (DEI) are essential to their businesses. To measure the success of their DEI programs, organizations must analyze data related to their workforce. This data can include demographic information on employees, employee satisfaction surveys, and performance assessments. Organizations need to analyze this data to identify potential employee diversity, equity, and inclusion issues.

Analyzing the data can also provide organizations with insights into their DEI goals and their progress over time. This can help organizations identify areas where they have been successful and areas where more work is needed. Measuring DEI goals can help organizations ensure they are achieving their desired outcomes and making progress toward their objectives. This information can also be used to assess the effectiveness of the organization's DEI programs and make necessary adjustments to ensure they meet their goals.

Organizations should measure the impact of their DEI efforts to understand the effectiveness of their DEI initiatives better. This data can provide insight into the organization's progress toward its DEI goals and objectives. Additionally, organizations should assess the diversity of their workforce to identify any areas of improvement. This data can help them create an equitable and inclusive workplace, understand underlying issues, and develop strategies to promote diversity and inclusion. Organizations should use the data they collect to evaluate current programs and initiatives. This will help them to identify any areas of success, as well as any areas of improvement. By understanding the strengths and weaknesses of their DEI programs, organizations can adjust their initiatives to ensure they are meeting their DEI goals. Additionally, organizations should use this data to develop new programs and initiatives that promote diversity and inclusion.

10.2 Collaborative Program Evaluation

The "Collaborative Program Evaluation Utilizing DEI Methods" approach is a comprehensive way of evaluating the success of organizational initiatives and programs. It takes into account the perspectives of all stakeholders, particularly those from underrepresented groups, in order to assess the effectiveness of these programs. This method is rooted in the DEI principles of Diversity, Equity, and Inclusion, which recognize the need for an inclusive and equitable workplace.

The approach seeks to understand how these programs are impacting different stakeholders from various backgrounds, and how they can be improved. It employs a range of DEI methods such as focus groups, surveys, interviews, and observation to collect feedback from a wide range of voices. This way, the evaluation process is more comprehensive and takes into account all the perspectives of the stakeholders, not just the dominant group. It can also help to identify and address any underlying issues that may be preventing the success of the initiatives and programs.

The collaborative program evaluation method is an effective way to measure the success of a program. It looks at both qualitative and quantitative data from different stakeholders to form a comprehensive evaluation of the initiative. Qualitative data is gathered from interviews, surveys, focus groups, and other methods to gain a better understanding of the experiences of the stakeholders. This data can then be used to identify any underlying issues that may be preventing the success of the program.

A comprehensive evaluation of the initiative should take into account both qualitative and quantitative data. Qualitative data, such as interviews, surveys, and focus groups, provides an understanding of the experiences of the stakeholders. This data can then be used to identify any underlying issues that may be preventing the success of the program.

Quantitative data, meanwhile, gives an understanding of the overall trends in the program outcomes. By analyzing this data, it is possible to determine the effectiveness of the program in achieving its goals. When both qualitative and quantitative data are used together, it provides a wide range of voices and perspectives. This helps to provide a more accurate assessment of the program, as all stakeholders are considered.

Measuring the effectiveness of a program is a complex process. To get a comprehensive view of its impact, it is important to consider both qualitative and quantitative data. This combination of data helps to create a more accurate assessment of the program, as it takes into account the perspectives of all stakeholders.

The DEI methods used in this approach create a safe and open space for stakeholders to express their experiences and perspectives. This helps to identify any disparities in program outcomes, as well as to assess the extent to which the program is meeting its objectives for DEI-related issues. This helps to ensure that the program is achieving its goals and is making progress towards creating an equitable and inclusive environment.

Analyzing the impact of a program requires the consideration of diverse viewpoints. To this end, DEI (Diversity, Equity, and Inclusion) methods provide a platform to capture the experiences and perspectives of stakeholders. Through the use of these methods, it is possible to identify any disparities in program outcomes and measure the extent to which the program is making progress on its DEI goals.

The data collected through DEI methods also helps inform future decisions related to the program. This is critical to ensure that the program meets its objectives and creates an equitable and inclusive environment. By considering both qualitative and quantitative data, program designers can make decisions based on a comprehensive view of the program's impact.

10.3 Developing Long-Term Strategies for Change

When it comes to developing long-term strategies for change, Diversity, Equity, and Inclusion (DEI) needs to be at the forefront of the conversation. DEI strategies should be implemented in all areas of the organization, from recruitment and hiring processes to the development of policies. This means that companies must create a culture where diversity and inclusion are seen as priorities.

Organizations need to take a proactive approach to implementing DEI strategies. This means ensuring that all employees are aware of the importance of diversity and inclusion and that they are provided with the resources and tools necessary to ensure their success. Companies should also ensure that they regularly evaluate their current policies and practices to ensure they meet the needs of their diverse workforce.

At the same time, organizations should also take steps to promote a safe and respectful environment for all employees. This could include things like providing training on unconscious bias and setting up a reporting system for any incidents of discrimination or harassment. Making sure that all employees are aware of and understand the DEI policies and guidelines is essential to creating a culture of inclusion and respect. Finally, organizations should strive to create an environment that celebrates diversity and encourages employees to bring their unique perspectives to the workplace.

Creating an inclusive workplace is essential to achieving a true culture of diversity and respect. Companies should focus on increasing diversity in their hiring process, but they should also look for ways to create an environment where everyone feels welcome and safe. Regular town hall meetings, creating safe spaces for employees to share their experiences, and providing Employee Resource Groups are all good starting points.

It is also important to ensure that all employees are aware of and understand the company's DEI policies and guidelines. Companies should create policies that focus on diversity, equity, and inclusion, such as anti-discrimination policies, diversity and inclusion initiatives, and unconscious bias training. These policies will help to ensure that employees are treated fairly and with respect, and are protected from any type of discrimination, prejudice, or harassment.

Organizations should strive to create a workplace that celebrates diversity and encourages employees to bring their unique perspectives and ideas. By creating a culture of inclusion, companies can foster an environment that is open to the different backgrounds and lifestyles of each employee. This will result in a more productive and creative workplace.

Creating a workplace that celebrates diversity and encourages employees to bring their unique perspectives is essential for a business to succeed. A culture of inclusion promotes the acceptance and appreciation of different backgrounds and lifestyles, resulting in a more productive and creative workplace.

Companies must monitor their DEI initiatives to ensure they are making progress. Recruitment and hiring processes should be regularly audited, and policies should be evaluated to determine how they are impacting staff. Benchmarking should be used to track progress in the right direction. Additionally, businesses should seek external partners to further foster diversity and inclusion. Taking these proactive steps can help organizations build a workplace that is diverse and supportive.

Conclusion

When attempting to foster diversity, equity, and inclusion (DEI) within the foundation of higher education, it is essential to understand the importance of actively implementing DEI perspectives. This means recognizing the various backgrounds, identities, and experiences of all members of the community. Additionally, it means providing the necessary resources and support for those who may not have access to the same opportunities as others.

Once this understanding is established, institutions must take the necessary steps to implement DEI initiatives. This includes the formation of DEI committees and the creation of DEI policies. These initiatives should be designed to promote and sustain an inclusive environment for all. Furthermore, these initiatives should be regularly reviewed and updated to ensure that they are effective and in alignment with the overall vision and mission of the institution.

Finally, a DEI perspective should be integrated into the curriculum of the institution. This can be achieved through the integration of DEI themes into lectures and the addition of DEI-focused classes. Doing this allows individuals to gain a broader understanding of the impact of DEI initiatives on the overall community. Additionally, it fosters the development of skills necessary to create an inclusive environment. By actively implementing DEI perspectives within the foundation of higher education.

Final Thoughts and Call to Action

When promoting diversity, equity, and inclusion (DEI) in an organization, the first step is acknowledging the need. Companies must recognize that DEI is not a box to check off but a continuous journey to create and sustain a workplace where all employees feel valued and respected and can reach their full potential. This requires commitment from the top—executive sponsors, and leaders must ensure their team is equipped and empowered to undertake DEI measures. It is also essential to have an articulated strategy outlining why DEI is necessary, the goals, and how they will be assessed. Finally, it is essential to have ongoing conversations and provide employees with the tools and resources needed to support their DEI initiatives. Ultimately, organizations need to remember that DEI is a long-term commitment, and all employees should be involved in creating an equitable work environment. It is not enough to provide training; instead, DEI must be woven into the fabric of the workplace, from hiring to onboarding new employees. Companies can only create and maintain a culture of equity and inclusion through this kind of sustained effort.

Companies must go beyond simply providing training to foster a culture of diversity, equity, and inclusion. Training is a significant first step in the right direction, but long-term success lies in integrating DEI into the workplace fabric. This means ensuring that DEI is part of the hiring process, onboarding new employees, and a part of the everyday culture. Companies should strive to ensure that DEI is woven into the various policies and procedures that are in place. This includes providing training on unconscious bias and creating a culture where employees feel comfortable discussing DEI.

Additionally, companies should be held accountable by setting measurable goals and tracking progress.

Through this sustained effort, organizations can create and maintain an environment of equity and inclusion.

Creating an environment where everyone feels safe to express their ideas and opinions is vital to a successful DEI initiative. Companies must ensure that they have policies and systems in place to protect employees from discrimination and harassment. Clear guidelines and expectations should be established and communicated to all employees. In addition, companies must provide training and resources to ensure that their employees are aware of and understand the importance of diversity and inclusion. This includes providing training on unconscious bias and creating a culture where employees feel comfortable discussing DEI. This helps promote a culture of inclusivity, respect, and understanding. Finally, companies should be accountable for their DEI initiatives by setting measurable goals and tracking progress. This helps ensure that DEI initiatives are making an impact and are not just lip service. Through this sustained effort, organizations can create and maintain an environment of equity and inclusion.

Creating an inclusive environment requires more than just a few initiatives; organizations must be willing to invest in DEI efforts and be proactive in their approach. Companies should take a stand against discrimination or prejudice and create a culture that respects and understands every workplace member. To ensure they succeed in their efforts, they need to set measurable goals and track progress to ensure their DEI initiatives are making an impact, not just lip service.

In addition, companies should strive to provide a safe and secure space for everyone, regardless of race, gender, sexual orientation, or any other aspect of identity. This means courageously speaking out against injustice and holding people accountable for their actions. It also means providing the necessary resources and training to ensure everyone knows their rights and responsibilities. By taking a stand for DEI, organizations can create a workplace where everyone feels valued, heard, and respected.

Appendices

Appendix A: To integrate DEI in higher education rapidly, follow these steps!

To integrate Diversity, Equity, and Inclusion (DEI) in higher education rapidly, follow these steps:

1. Assess the Current State: Conduct an assessment to determine the current level of DEI in your institution. This may include examining policies, practices, and demographics, as well as surveying students, faculty, and staff to understand their experiences and perspectives.

2. Set Strategic Goals: Develop clear, measurable, and time-bound goals that align with your institution's mission and values. These goals should prioritize creating an inclusive and equitable learning environment and improving representation and diversity across all levels.

3. Allocate Resources: Dedicate financial and human resources to support DEI initiatives. This may involve creating an office or committee responsible for DEI, hiring staff with expertise in this area, or providing training and development opportunities.

4. Review and Revise Policies: Evaluate existing policies and procedures to identify areas where bias or inequity may be present. Make necessary revisions, such as updating recruitment and admission strategies, implementing more inclusive curriculum frameworks, and revising evaluation and promotion criteria.

5. Increase Representation and Access: Develop strategies to attract and retain underrepresented students, faculty, and staff. This could include targeted recruitment efforts,

providing financial aid and scholarships, and offering mentoring and support programs.

6. Provide Training and Education: Conduct mandatory training sessions and workshops for faculty, staff, and students to enhance understanding and awareness of diversity, equity, and inclusion. Offer ongoing professional development programs to promote best practices in teaching, research, and administration.

7. Foster Inclusive Campus Culture: Encourage dialogue and engagement around DEI topics within the campus community. Support the creation of student-led organizations, clubs, and events that celebrate diversity and promote inclusivity. Promote an inclusive work environment for faculty and staff through policies and resources.

8. Evaluate and Monitor Progress: Regularly assess the effectiveness of DEI initiatives and programs by collecting and analyzing data on student success, faculty and staff diversity, and campus climate. Adjust strategies if needed, based on the findings.

9. Collaborate and Learn from Others: Engage with other higher education institutions, professional organizations, and community partners to share best practices and learn from their experiences in implementing DEI initiatives rapidly.

10. Communicate and Engage: Ensure transparency and open communication throughout the entire process. Regularly update the campus community on progress, celebrate successes, and address concerns or challenges openly and honestly.

Remember, implementing DEI initiatives is an ongoing process that requires continuous commitment and engagement from all stakeholders in the institution.

www.ingramcontent.com/pod-product-compliance
Lightning Source LLC
Chambersburg PA
CBHW041811110726
48006CB00019B/2347